# Praise for the
# Happy Herbivore Series

"*Happy Herbivore Holidays & Gatherings* provides you with simple recipes to share the joy of great-tasting, healthy cuisine with your friends and family. It's a go-to resource for those special occasions, or for anytime!"

—BRIAN WENDEL, *FORKS OVER KNIVES*

"Somehow, Lindsay Nixon has done it again. Her food is healthy, familiar, easy, and delicious. You'll eat this food simply for the joy of eating, but will be bettering your health at the same time. Of all the prescriptions I give to my patients, Lindsay's cookbooks are among the most important."

—THOMAS M. CAMPBELL, MD, COAUTHOR OF THE BESTSELLING *THE CHINA STUDY* AND AUTHOR, *THE CAMPBELL PLAN*

"Lindsay Nixon's FIFTH cookbook answers everyone's question: Whatever can I cook for holidays and special occasions that is delicious and still plant based and with no oil? Her satisfying and innovative recipes here will make each holiday and special occasion absolutely memorable."

—CALDWELL B. ESSELSTYN, JR., MD AND ANN CRILE ESSELSTYN, AUTHOR OF *PREVENT AND REVERSE HEART DISEASE*

"Lindsay Nixon adds her newest cookbook, this one for your holiday planning of the big family feast. It's the day of bounty and feast with family and friends that we cherish, and this usually means consuming rich foods. But, in this case, we can walk away from the table with health—and what better way to enjoy life with family and friends. Give this book a try and you will see for yourself."

—T. COLIN AND KAREN CAMPBELL, CENTER FOR NUTRITION STUDIES

"Lindsay continues to hit it out of the plant-strong park with her latest edition of delicious, party happy, Happy Herbivore recipes."

—RIP ESSELSTYN, *NEW YORK TIMES* BESTSELLING AUTHOR OF *MY BEEF WITH MEAT*

"Lindsay Nixon and I had similar childhoods in ways that count—we both came from families where food was the focus of every celebration. We have both watched mothers and aunties and grandmothers spend all day in the kitchen preparing for every holiday and preparing every dish with love. Lindsay brings all that love and every joyful memory with her into this, her latest cookbook, *Happy Herbivore Holidays & Gatherings*, and better yet, she does it with delicious, healthy plant-based meals that we can all embrace."

**—DEL SROUFE, AUTHOR OF *BETTER THAN VEGAN* AND *FORKS OVER KNIVES—THE COOKBOOK***

"Lindsay's newest book exceeds all of our expectations for creative holiday meals. Meals you make for your family and friends from *Happy Herbivore Holidays & Gatherings* will speak louder than words about the many reasons to eat healthy foods."

**—JOHN AND MARY MCDOUGALL, BESTSELLING AUTHORS AND FOUNDERS OF THE MCDOUGALL PROGRAM**

# More books in Lindsay S. Nixon's Happy Herbivore Series

The Happy Herbivore Cookbook

Everyday Happy Herbivore

Happy Herbivore Abroad

Happy Herbivore Light & Lean

Happy Herbivore Guide to
Plant-Based Living (e-book only)

# HAPPY HERBIVORE
## Holidays & Gatherings

# HAPPY
# HERBIVORE
## Holidays & Gatherings

*Easy Plant-Based Recipes for Your*
*Healthiest Celebrations and Special Occasions*

## LINDSAY S. NIXON

BENBELLA BOOKS, INC.
DALLAS, TX

Nutritional information for each recipe was computed using caloriecount.com. Each analysis provided is per serving. Unless otherwise noted, optional ingredients are not included, and when a recipe calls for multiple amounts, e.g., three to four garlic cloves, the lesser amount is computed. For nondairy milk, unsweetened almond milk was used in the calculation. Breads and buns are not included in the nutritional analysis (see packaging for that information). Sodium content is also not included because values are significantly different between brands and because the calculator tools have too much discrepancy with sodium values to provide a safe and reliable estimate.

BenBella

BenBella Books, Inc.
10300 N. Central Expressway, Suite #530
Dallas, TX 75231
www.benbellabooks.com
Send feedback to feedback@benbellabooks.com

Printed in the United States of America
10 9 8 7 6 5 4 3 2 1

Library of Congress Cataloging-in-Publication Data
Nixon, Lindsay S., author.
  Happy herbivore holidays & gatherings : easy plant-based recipes for your healthiest celebrations
and special occasions / by Lindsay S. Nixon.
      pages cm
  Includes bibliographical references and index.
  ISBN 978-1-940363-26-4 (paperback) — ISBN 978-1-940363-65-3 (electronic)  1.  Vegan cooking.  2.
Holiday cooking.  3.  Entertaining.  I.  Title.  II.  Title: Happy herbivore holidays and gatherings.
  TX837.N576 2014
  641.5'636—dc23
                           2014009078

Editing by Debbie Harmsen, Kellie Coppola, and
   Vy Tran
Copyediting by Shannon Kelly
Proofreading by Kristin Vorce and Amy Zarkos
Indexing by Clive Pyne, Book Indexing Services
Text design by Faceout Studio
Text composition by Kit Sweeney
Printed by Versa Press
Cover design by Faceout Studio

Cover photo and photos on pages xi, xii, 4, 15,
   37, 72, 84, 87, 130, 156, 164, 186, 187 by Natala
   Constantine
Interior food photography by Jackie Sobon
Interior food prep work photography by Ira Mintz
Photos on pages 93, 115, and 189 (top) by Neely Roberts
Photo on page 35 by Ruby Ernst
Photo on page 155 by Kel Elwood Photography
Additional photography by Lindsay S. Nixon

Distributed by Perseus Distribution (www.perseusdistribution.com)
To place orders through Perseus Distribution:
Tel: (800) 343-4499    Fax: (800) 351-5073    E-mail: orderentry@perseusbooks.com

SIGNIFICANT DISCOUNTS FOR BULK SALES ARE AVAILABLE.
PLEASE CONTACT GLENN YEFFETH AT GLENN@BENBELLABOOKS.COM OR (214) 750-3628.

To my family and friends

# CONTENTS

# A WORD FROM LINDSAY

Break out your fancy pants! *Happy Herbivore Holidays & Gatherings* is an all-out celebration of food, family, friends, holidays, health, and love—*la dolce vita!*

Anytime my family comes together, a feast is sure to follow. Growing up, I loved holiday dinners crammed around my Aunt Carol's extended table with my parents, grandparents, and all my aunts, uncles, and cousins. It looked a little like a scene from *My Big Fat Greek Wedding*, but that was us: elbowing each other and arguing over who got the last meatball.

Perhaps what stayed with me the most was how much care and love my grandmother and Aunt Carol put into every dish. For them, cooking was an expression of their love. They would slave away all day, sometimes a few days in a row, preparing an elaborate celebratory meal big enough to feed our large family.

I still vividly remember waking up to the smell of meatballs at 7:00 a.m. (yes, 7:00 a.m.!) because my grandmother was already working on our Christmas dinner. To this day, my Aunt Carol still gets up at around 6:00 a.m. to start cooking on major holidays. In my family, food is love and cooking is an expression of that love!

I saw this same kind of love and passion in my mom's best friend, my "Aunt" Joan. Aunt Joan is not only an amazing cook, she absolutely *loves* to cook. Every meal is a celebration of life!

As I grew older, I dreamed of the day I could throw amazing dinner parties like Aunt Joan. I wanted to be her. I wanted to be the kind of person that everyone called a good cook, the person everyone wanted a dinner invite from—whether it was for an intimate dinner party, a fun barbecue, a casual home-cooked meal, an elaborate holiday feast, or a festive New Year's Eve bash. I wanted to be a domestic goddess, or at least pass for one sometimes!

Yet for years I was doubtful that would ever happen. The one time I tried to cook a nice dinner in college, it was so bad that my friends ragged on me for years to come. I found the nerve to try cooking again as a newlywed, and while that meal wasn't *inedible*, it was hardly worth all the time and effort I'd spent. At that point I started to wonder if I was born missing some culinary link in my DNA.

As a result, my husband did most of the cooking in our marriage—that is, until I went plant-based. Vegetarian he could handle, but when I switched to a whole foods, plant-based diet (completely eliminating oil and all animal products, including dairy and eggs), he was lost. I knew if I was going to eat, I had to make it myself, so I stumbled back into the kitchen.

I was delighted to discover I had a real love and passion for cooking healthy foods. Today, I'm happiest in my kitchen, preparing foods for those I love. Serving others is like giving them a great big hug! I frequently host dinner parties, big event parties, and parties for no reason but to have a party. I also find myself feeding friends who drop by. (Conveniently, they are always hungry when they ring the doorbell!)

Recently, my mother posted to Facebook that she was flying to California to visit me . . . and that I had agreed to do all the cooking. (Nice play, Mom.) I hadn't said anything of the sort, but I was happy to cook for her nonetheless, and it was a real honor, too. My mother has never let someone else do all the cooking, except for her mother (my late grandmother, mentioned earlier).

This is where my cooking, and this book, comes from. For me, cooking is a celebration of life and love. *Happy Herbivore Holidays & Gatherings* is about cooking for life's special moments of togetherness (even if you don't love cooking), with health, happiness, and heavenly deliciousness in mind.

**Together we will make your next holiday or gathering a special one. You and your dazzling dishes can be the life of the party!**

In this cookbook, I bring in the classics plus some new edgy dishes with foolproof recipes to help you cook with confidence all year long. And since I, too, want to be the life of the party, I've made sure these recipes won't bog us down in the kitchen. Every dish is easy enough for a weeknight and guaranteed to impress!

Celebrate the sweet life with me,

# The Pre-Party

## Planning for Big Meals & Celebrations

I love to cook, but I don't love spending all day in the kitchen—I have family and friends to socialize with! (And puzzles to put together—that's my holiday thing.) But when you're cooking big feasts or multidish meals, it can be challenging to get *out* of the kitchen. How do you find the balance? *And how do you get everything on the table at the same time while it's still hot?*

The secret, which I learned from Ina Garten's book *Barefoot Contessa Foolproof: Recipes You Can Trust*, is to have a cooking game plan. Before the big day, think about the components of each recipe, as well the total cook time, and consider what, if anything, can or should be made ahead. For example, when I'm making potato salad, I know I have to cook my potatoes first and that they need time to chill before I can prepare my salad. This means I tend

to make my potatoes a day or so before or, if nothing else, first thing in the morning so they can chill all afternoon and I can assemble my potato salad just before dinner. Similarly, at Thanksgiving, I always make cranberry sauce a few days ahead. Cranberry sauce needs several hours to chill anyway, so making it a few days ahead takes one more item off the list. Garten also recommends getting as specific as possible in your game plan (e.g., noting "5:30 p.m.: preheat the oven") and laying out every recipe and component step by step.

Although planning ahead sounds tricky, once you follow my steps and implement the game plan system, you'll see it makes cooking—and entertaining—a breeze.

By thinking about each dish and the components involved, you can organize the cooking so every delicious dish is ready at the very moment you want to serve dinner. I have to be my own chef, sous chef, dish-washer, hostess, and server (okay, my

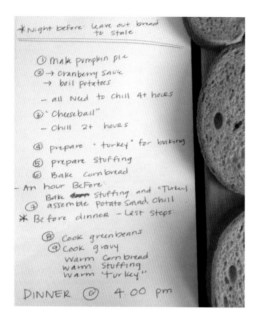

*My master plan for Thanksgiving*

husband helps sometimes!), so getting my plan organized on paper and out of my head makes entertaining infinitely less stressful and way more enjoyable. Try using a game plan once and I promise you'll never cook a big meal without one again!

## CREATING YOUR GAME PLAN

1. Choose your recipes. What are you serving? For ease, I've included comprehensive menus for a dozen special occasions as well as menu suggestions for everyday occasions (see "Dinner Party Menus" in the appendix) in this book. You'll also find additional recipe suggestions from my other cookbooks for holidays and events all year long (see "More

Holiday Menus" in the appendix). Build your perfect menu!

2. Examine the recipes, paying close attention to the steps required for each component. Is there anything that can, or should, be made ahead to save time? For example, grains, such as rice or quinoa, can be made in advance. Potatoes, for mashing or potato salad, along with many desserts, can also be made ahead. The same is true for squashes—you can roast or cook any squash a few days in advance. If you aren't able to make these items a day or two before, schedule them first thing in the morning.

3. Once your components are taken care of, look to the total cook time of each recipe. Which recipes take the most time to cook or prep? The least time? For those going in the oven, are the temperatures different or the same? Can anything go in together? Generally, you want to list dishes in the order of longest cook time (e.g., vegan meatloaf) to shortest cook time (e.g., gravy).

4. Once the recipe order is complete, work backwards from when you want dinner to be ready, writing down the time you're going to prep and make each item. It can also help to add estimates for prep time, cook time, and finishing time next to each step. (e.g., 5:00 p.m.: assemble vegan meatloaf, prep time: 15 minutes, 5:15 p.m.:

bake meatloaf, cook time: 50-60 minutes, finishes: 6:10 p.m.). Throw-together dishes like salads can usually be worked in wherever you have a gap of time, or assemble them quickly before serving.

5. Lastly, clear extra space in your fridge for the big day. You'll need room for foods requiring time to chill.

## PRESENTING YOUR BOUNTY

There are a few different ways you can serve your guests, and which style you select may depend on the type of occasion, the party space or venue, the total number of guests, or who the guests are. (For example, are you dealing with picky eaters or an array of different dietary needs?) If you want to be ultra–fancy pants (and your guests can generally eat the same foods), serve each person restaurant-style, either in courses or with their plate containing a serving of each item at the onset. This is my favorite approach (it's so classy!), but it does take a little extra work, since you're doing all the plating and serving. You also may need to do a little more thoughtful planning with your menu, making sure all of your dishes are suitable for everyone's dietary needs.

If you find yourself with a limited amount of food (maybe something went awry or you suddenly realized your food shrank during cooking . . . or you grossly underestimated how much you'd need—been there done that!)—pre-plating can save the day. Serv-

ing restaurant-style will ensure that every guest gets a serving of each delightful dish you make. (Plus I know I'm guilty of taking gigantic portions when serving myself. My eyes are absolutely bigger than my stomach.)

An additional benefit to the restaurant-style approach is that it helps with space: if your seating area is small or you'll be cramming a lot of people around a table, serving restaurant-style saves table space and keeps things comfortable. However, another option for small dining spaces is serving buffet-style, where guests take a plate and go through a line of your goodies, helping themselves to whichever menu items they want. This is great for big parties

## THINK IN COLOR

Color equals satisfaction. The more color on a plate, the more abundant your meal feels. (A plate of beige may be delicious, but it doesn't feed our eyes.) This is a sneaky trick to keep in mind with skeptical guests. We eat with our eyes first, so always take care to pick recipes with different colors. One of my mantras (and hashtags) is #tastetherealrainbow.

Appetizing Parties section (p. 66) for ideas on what to prepare for parties with this type of food presentation in mind.

with lots of guests, or when you'll be entertaining people with many different dietary needs. Each partygoer can create his or her own perfect plate. (I'm especially fond of buffet-style serving at outdoor parties, and it's a necessity at potlucks.) Buffet-style can be elegant or very casual—see the Party Bars section in this book for ideas on what types of food to include in buffet lines for different occasions.

Another option is family-style dining. Having your bounty in the center of the table makes your table colorful, and it allows guests to easily reach for seconds. Having guests passing serving bowls and plates around the table to each other also makes for a more special and intimate experience—the perfect ambiance for the holidays.

And of course let's not forget the most fuss-free option of all: grazing-style, where you have finger foods and other easy grab-and-eat snacks in serving dishes throughout the party area. See the Tailgating &

## GOODY BAGS

Remember childhood parties where you left with a present? I'm all about "goody bags" at my parties—send guests home with a meal for the next day! (This is also a great way to make sure leftovers leave your kitchen!) If you want to impress, serve soup in a mason jar, then tie a colored ribbon around it that captures the holiday you're celebrating!

# HOW TO USE THE ICONS IN THIS BOOK

| Q | GF | SF | MA | PA | P |

**QUICK** Recipes that come together in 30 minutes or less. Some recipes may require multitasking to complete in 30 minutes.

**GLUTEN FREE** Recipes that don't require wheat or barley. I can't vouch for every ingredient, though, so if you have an allergy or sensitivity, please make sure every ingredient you use is certified gluten free. For example, while oats themselves do not contain gluten, they may be cross-contaminated. Recipes with an asterisk next to the icon can be made gluten-free with simple substitutions. For example, use gluten-free tamari or coconut aminos in place of soy sauce. In non-baking recipes, rice flour is a fairly good replacement for whole-wheat flour.

**SOY FREE** Recipes that don't require tofu or tempeh. Recipes with an asterisk next to the icon can be made soy free with simple substitutions. For example, use coconut aminos in place of soy sauce, chickpea miso when miso is called for, and almond milk instead of soy milk.

**MAKE AHEAD** Recipes that can be made ahead for easier planning and prep.

**PREP AHEAD** Recipes that can be started (or prepped) ahead, but need a final step (such as baking or heating) the day of for best results. A **STOP** icon is included with each recipe to indicate where to stop your prep work.

**PORTABLE** Recipes that will travel well by car or train.

# Occasions

# Thanksgiving

I cook a feast on Thanksgiving, with the keyword being *feast*. Every year, without fail, I make way more food than I (and my guests) could ever eat. I can't help it. I also stuff myself to the point of total discomfort trying to eat it all. (Maybe I'll learn my lesson next year!)

Although Thanksgiving is about *gratitude*, it's also the biggest food holiday of the year. Thanksgiving is practically synonymous with turkey, leaving open the question: what do vegetarians and plant eaters ... *eat*?

Thanksgiving is the one holiday my beloved Herbies get a little stressed over (I start getting frantic e-mails about the big day in July!) and I get why. I, too, was scratching my head my first Thanksgiving as a vegetarian (I simply ate all the sides). I've since created my own lavish menu, and as the years have passed, I've come to love my family's plant-based Thanksgivings even more. Not only is our Thanksgiving about family and gratitude, it's about compassion and health, too.

Even better, our dinner plates have transformed into works of art, with so many different textures and brilliant colors. Beige is out! Vibrant is in!

Interestingly, my parents had their first plant-based Thanksgiving at my house, when they were still omnivores. I was up against more than sixty-five years of tradition, and endless teasing about going to the neighbor's house to sneak some turkey, but both of my parents were pleasantly surprised by their experience.

"I don't feel that we missed any of the traditional meal," my mom said. "It had all the flavors and taste of a traditional meal but it was healthy and fresh and vegan."

After going for seconds, my dad remarked, "I had no idea you could have everything we'd always had, just healthy and vegan. . . . It was a really good replica. I don't feel like I missed anything. It was really good!"

I find that the more years I'm plant-based, the more I move away from "traditional" replicas and into more edgy, "plant-proud" dishes like Stuffed Acorn Squash (p. 24). On the other hand, there's a certain comfort and enjoyment in familiarity, especially when you're serving others, so I always keep one or two traditional dishes in the mix, such as mashed potatoes or stuffing for sides and pumpkin pie for dessert.

On the next page you'll find my basic, crowd-pleasing menu for Thanksgiving. It features a celebratory centerpiece (the Thanksgiving Loaf) with all the sides and trimmings you expect and love! No bird? No problem!

**APPETIZER**

Butternut Soup (p. 12)

**MAIN DISH**

Thanksgiving Loaf (p. 15)

**SIDES**

mashed potatoes (p. 18)

Everyday Mushroom
 Gravy (p. 16)
Thanksgiving Gravy (p. 16)
Skillet Green Bean
 Casserole (p. 19)
Cornbread (p. 19)
Traditional Stuffing (p. 20)
Cranberry Sauce (p. 23)

Sweet Potato Casserole
 (p. 23)

**DESSERT**

Pumpkin Pie (p. 24)
Pumpkin Cheesecake (p. 26)

**MENU FOR ONE OR TWO**

Here's a special menu for those times when you're invited to a Thanksgiving potluck or celebration with omnivores and need to make your own plant-based Thanksgiving meal—or when it's an intimate Thanksgiving with just you and another.

Stuffed Acorn Squash (p. 24)
steamed vegetables or
 mashed potatoes and
 gravy (p. 18)
Mini Pumpkin Pies (p. 27)

For your side dish, steam some green beans or broccoli. Alternatively or in addition, whip up a small portion of mashed potatoes (see "Mashed Potatoes a Dozen Ways," p. 18) with Thanksgiving Gravy (p. 16) or Everyday Mushroom Gravy (p. 16).

# Butternut Soup

SERVES 2-4 | **GF** | **SF** | **MA** | **P** |

*I can't help myself. I have to include a butternut soup in every cookbook I write. This recipe is my new favorite, and it's a little edgy for Thanksgiving. If you want to go a bit more traditional, skip the chilies and lime, and add cinnamon (or pumpkin pie spice) to taste with a light drizzle of maple syrup. Or if you don't want a sweet, pumpkin-pie-tasting soup, add mild curry powder to taste—yes! Just three ingredients!* Ka-pow!

    1   butternut squash
  2-4   c vegetable broth
    1   4-oz can green chilies
  1-2   limes

1. Preheat oven to 375°F.
2. Slice squash in half lengthwise and place cut side down on a cookie sheet. Bake until fork-tender and skin is starting to brown (about 30–40 minutes).
3. Once cool enough to handle, scoop out and discard seeds. Then scoop flesh away from skin and transfer to a blender, working in batches if necessary.
4. Blend squash with broth as necessary to achieve a silky smooth soup consistency. Then blend in green chilies.
5. Reheat the soup on low on the stovetop if necessary.
6. Season with salt and pepper if desired. Squeeze fresh lime juice over top before serving.

**Per serving (serving 2):** 133 calories, 0.2g fat, 34g carbohydrates, 4.3g fiber, 7.8g sugars, 2.2g protein

# Thanksgiving Loaf

SERVES 4 | **GF** | **SF\*** | **MA** | **PA** | **P** |

*I've never had Tofurkey, and while my family has become pretty adventurous over the years, no amount of persuasion is going to get them to eat tofu shaped into a turkey mold. (Just sayin'.) If you want a centerpiece to your meal that doesn't pretend to be turkey, this Thanksgiving Loaf is where it's at. While this loaf doesn't taste anything like meatloaf (or turkey), it captures all the Thanksgiving flavors that we know and love.*

| | |
|---|---|
| 1 | 15-oz can white beans, drained and rinsed |
| 1 | c mashed potatoes (p. 18) |
| 1 | carrot |
| 1 | parsnip (optional) |
| 2 | celery stalks |
| 1 | small onion |
| 2½ | tbsp poultry seasoning (*not* powdered) |
| ½ | tsp rubbed sage (*not* powdered) |
| 2–3 | tbsp nutritional yeast |
| 2–3 | tbsp yellow miso* |
| ¾ | c instant oats (uncooked) |

1. Preheat oven to 350°F and set aside a standard loaf pan.
2. Pulse beans in a food processor or mash in a bowl with a fork so no whole beans are left, but mixture is still chunky with some bean parts. Transfer to a mixing bowl along with the mashed potatoes and set aside.
3. Grate, chop, or pulse vegetables in a food processor until finely minced, but do not puree. Add to mixing bowl with seasonings, nutritional yeast, and miso, stirring to combine.
4. Stir in oats and taste, adding additional nutritional yeast or miso if desired. **STOP**
5. Transfer combined mixture to your loaf pan, pat down firmly, and bake for 30–40 minutes until firmer and crisp on the top (make sure it's not still wet).
6. Let cool in the pan for 10–20 minutes before serving out of it (while keeping it perfectly intact).

▸▸▸ **CHEF'S NOTES:**

- *One-use aluminum loaf pans that have ridges on the sides make the prettiest loaves, and it's easier to pop the loaf out of that (and keep it perfectly intact) than a traditional metal pan. While normally I'd prefer not to use something that creates waste, I like a perfect, magazine-looking loaf at Thanksgiving.*
- *If using a regular pan, run a knife along the edges, put a plate or cutting board over top, flip over, and pat (bang) the bottom of the pan until your loaf slides out onto the plate or cutting board.*

**Per serving (¼ loaf):** 259 calories, 2.5g fat, 48g carbohydrates, 11.5g fiber, 3.9g sugars, 13g protein

# Everyday Mushroom Gravy

HOLIDAY HIT

MAKES 1 CUP | **Q** | **GF\*** | **SF\*** | **PA** |

*This recipe from* Everyday Happy Herbivore *is, hands down, the fan-favorite gravy. Because this is also the gravy my parents serve at their Thanksgiving, I'm including it here as an alternative to the Thanksgiving Gravy.*

    1   c water
    2   tbsp low-sodium soy sauce*
    2   tbsp nutritional yeast, divided
    ¼   tsp onion powder
    ¼   tsp garlic powder
    ¼   tsp ground ginger
    8   oz white or brown mushrooms, sliced
        Italian seasoning as needed
    ½   c nondairy milk
    2   tbsp cornstarch
        a couple of dashes of ground nutmeg
        (optional) (see note)

1. In a skillet, whisk water with low-sodium soy sauce, 1 tbsp of nutritional yeast, onion powder, garlic powder, and ground ginger.
2. Bring to a boil and add mushrooms, sprinkling them generously with Italian seasoning (a good 10 shakes).
3. Continue to sauté over medium-high heat until the mushrooms are brown and soft, about 3 minutes. Meanwhile, whisk nondairy milk with cornstarch and remaining 1 tbsp of nutritional yeast. Add a very light dash of nutmeg, if desired.
4. Pour nondairy milk mixture over mushrooms, stirring to combine. `STOP` Reduce heat to low and continue to cook until thick and gravy-like, about 5 minutes.
5. Add black pepper to taste (I like it really peppery) and a few more shakes of Italian seasoning unless you were very generous before. Taste again, adding a pinch of salt if necessary.
6. Set aside for a few minutes to let the flavors merge before serving.

▶▶▶ **CHEF'S NOTE:**

*For a smoky-flavored gravy, substitute smoked paprika for the nutmeg, adding more to taste.*

Per serving (¼ c): 60 calories, 1.4g fat, 8.9g carbohydrates, 1.4g fiber, 1.2g sugars, 5.6g protein

# Thanksgiving Gravy

MAKES 1 CUP | **Q** | **GF\*** | **SF\*** | **PA** |

*I designed this gravy specifically for Thanksgiving when I wrote my first cookbook,* The Happy Herbivore Cookbook. *It captures all the Thanksgiving flavors you know and love while complementing basic sides like green beans, mashed potatoes, or grains.*

    ¼   c nutritional yeast
    ¼   c white whole-wheat flour*
    1   c nondairy milk
    1   small onion, diced
    8   oz white mushrooms, thinly sliced
    2   tbsp low-sodium soy sauce*
    1   tsp rubbed sage (*not* powdered)

1. Whisk nutritional yeast and flour together with nondairy milk and set aside.
2. Line a large frying pan with a thin layer of water and cook onion and mushrooms over high heat until the mushrooms start to soften and turn brown and most of the water has evaporated.
3. Add milk mixture, soy sauce, and sage to the pan, stirring to combine. `STOP`
4. Bring to a boil and continue to cook until thick.
5. Add salt and pepper to taste.

Per serving (¼ c): 70 calories, 1g fat, 10.9g carbohydrates, 2.6g fiber, 3.3g sugars, 6.1g protein

Thanksgiving Gravy

# MASHED POTATOES
# A DOZEN WAYS

No one really needs a recipe for mashed potatoes (you just mash up some potatoes!), but since mashed potatoes are, quite possibly, my favorite food, I've learned a number of different ways to make them.

Before I was plant-based, I made mashed potatoes with milk, as most people do, so when I went plant-based, I started making my mashed potatoes with soy milk (or almond milk) and happily discovered it worked just as well.

If I'm not going to drown my mashed potatoes in gravy, I find that generous amounts of garlic powder and onion powder (the finely granulated kind, not the coarse mince or powdery-floury kinds), makes them plenty flavorful, without adding butter or a vegan butter substitute like margarine. (I add salt and black pepper, too, of course!)

I also (and trust me on this one!) love adding Dijon mustard to plain mashed potatoes. In fact, anytime I'm serving Portobello Steaks (p. 86) or asparagus, I make my Dijon mashed potatoes. (A little goes a long way, so add Dijon to taste and omit other spices.)

Another option is adding nutritional yeast, which makes the potatoes a bit cheesy. My latest discovery, however, is vegetable broth. I ran out of both soy and almond milk on Thanksgiving last year and, not wanting to forgo serving mashed potatoes to my in-laws, I used vegetable broth and found it makes for an incredible mashed potato. (Broth and nutritional yeast are even more amazing coupled together! My No-Chicken Broth [p. 168] or the powder base really kicks it up notch!)

I shared my broth discovery on Happy Herbivore's Facebook page and learned of yet another delicious trick from my fans: use the cooking water from boiling the potatoes! The starchy cooking water makes mashed potatoes even creamier.

If you're looking for a less starchy mashed potato experience, use cauliflower. Or find a middle ground and use both cauliflower and potatoes. I often oven-roast garlic and cauliflower (place on a cookie sheet lined with parchment paper and bake at 375°F for 20–25 minutes, flipping halfway), and then slip that into my mashed potatoes for a more "rustic" mashed potato.

You can also add beans! Try whipping a can of white beans into your mashed potatoes, with (or without) a little fresh rosemary. A pinch or two of lemon zest and/or a little bit of lemon juice makes this version perfect for a spring meal.

Speaking of spring, for Passover specifically, mix prepared white horseradish into plain mashed potatoes to taste and garnish with fresh chives.

Cooked parsnips are another great addition to mashed potatoes (double veggie points!) and if you slip in some cooked cabbage or kale, you have colcannon, a traditional Irish dish.

For mashed sweet potatoes, use soy or almond milk, plus cinnamon (or pumpkin pie spice) to taste. Or make Sweet Potato Casserole (p. 23).

**Potatoes not to use:** waxy potatoes, such as Yukon Gold potatoes, especially if you plan to use an electric beater—you'll end up with glue! My go-to choice is the little red-skin potatoes (they're a touch sweet!) or Idaho or russet potatoes, though if you want a smooth mashed potato consistency, steam the latter instead of boiling them.

# Skillet Green Bean Casserole

SERVES 2 | **Q** | **GF** | **SF** | **MA** | **P** |

*I didn't grow up eating green bean casserole, but I remember it being advertised on television. This ultimately led me to asking my mom to make it every year, which then led her to say, "Why? You don't like mushrooms. Or onions. Or creamy things, Lindsay!" (I happen to love all those foods now and this casserole, too!)*

- 1 c vegetable broth, divided
- 1 onion, diced
- 2 garlic cloves, minced
- 1 c mushrooms, thinly sliced
- ½ lb green beans, trimmed
- 1 tbsp poultry seasoning (granulated, not powdered) (see note)
- 1 tbsp Dijon mustard
- ½ tsp dried thyme
- ½ tsp rubbed sage (*not* powdered)
  dash of nutmeg
- ½ c nondairy milk
- 2 tbsp nutritional yeast
- 1 tbsp cornstarch
  toasted bread crumbs (optional)
  fried onions (optional)

1. Line a large skillet with a thin layer of broth and sauté the onion and garlic over high heat until onion is translucent, about a minute.
2. Reduce heat to medium and add the remaining broth plus mushrooms, green beans, poultry seasoning, Dijon mustard, thyme, sage, and a dash of nutmeg, stirring to coat the mushrooms with seasonings.
3. Continue to cook until the mushrooms are soft and the green beans are cooked but still crisp, about 7 minutes.
4. Meanwhile, in a measuring glass or small bowl, whisk nondairy milk with nutritional yeast and cornstarch.
5. Once green beans and mushrooms are cooked, pour in the nondairy milk mixture. Stir a few times and allow the mixture to thicken.
6. Once it thickens slightly, turn off heat. Add salt and pepper to taste, then spoon the casserole mixture into bowls and top with toasted bread crumbs and fried onions if desired.

▶▶▶ **CHEF'S NOTE:**
*In a pinch, you can use Italian seasoning instead of poultry seasoning.*

**Per serving:** 145 calories, 2g fat, 26.9g carbohydrates, 8.5g fiber, 5.1g sugars, 9.2g protein

**VARIATION**
**Asparagus Casserole:** *Replace green beans with asparagus for a tasty alternative!*

# Cornbread

SERVES 9 | **Q** | **GF\*** | **SF** | **MA** | **P** |

*You may recognize this cornbread recipe from my previous cookbooks. It's a favorite and for good reason: you need*

*Cornbread continued...*

only a handful of pantry staples to make it happen, and it's foolproof. You can also get a little fancy pants by adding corn (fire-roasted is my favorite), sliced jalapeño, or diced bell pepper in the batter or sprinkled on top.

> 1   c yellow cornmeal
> 1   c white whole-wheat flour*
> 1   tbsp baking powder
> 1   c nondairy milk
> ¼   c unsweetened applesauce
> ¼   c pure maple syrup or agave nectar (see note)
> 2   tbsp raw sugar (optional)
>     Your choice of add-ins (optional)

1. Preheat oven to 400°F and set aside a 9-inch glass dish or nonstick square baking pan. (I also love a springform pan for this recipe.)
2. In a mixing bowl, whisk cornmeal, flour, and baking powder together.
3. Add nondairy milk, applesauce, maple syrup or agave nectar, and sugar, if using.
4. Stir a few times, add in optional ingredients, if using, and then stir until just combined.
5. Pour batter into pan and bake for approximately 20 minutes—you want it to be golden, starting to crack, and firm to the touch.
6. When a toothpick is inserted in the center, it should come out clean.

▶▶▶ **CHEF'S NOTES:**

- *Replace 2 tbsp of the maple syrup with 2–3 tbsp of additional nondairy milk for a less sweet cornbread.*
- *For a gluten-free cornbread, substitute gluten-free all-purpose flour blend for the whole-wheat flour.*

**Per serving:** 131 calories, 1g fat, 28.7g carbohydrates, 1.6g fiber, 6g sugars, 2.6g protein

# Traditional Stuffing

SERVES 8  | **Q** | **SF** | **PA** |

*I created this recipe for the two men in my life who live and die for stuffing at Thanksgiving. (I'm talking to you, Dad and hubby!)*

> 6    slices of whole-wheat bread
> 1    c vegetable broth, divided
> 1    medium onion, chopped
> 4    celery stalks, sliced or diced
> 2–3  tbsp Italian seasoning

1. Leave bread out overnight so it becomes stale (if you forget, toast it, but stale is best).
2. Preheat oven to 350°F.
3. Cube bread.
4. Line a skillet with a thin layer of broth and sauté onion and celery until onion is translucent and all the liquid has cooked off. Set aside to cool.
5. In your casserole or baking dish, toss bread cubes with 2 tbsp Italian seasoning. Stir in cooked onion and celery and add more seasoning if desired. (Go on, give it a taste!) `STOP`
6. Drizzle with ¼ cup broth and bake for 30 minutes.
7. Check every 10 minutes and add more broth as necessary to prevent stuffing from drying out. (I find the preferred "wetness" of stuffing varies from family to family—do what you like!)

**Per serving:** 70 calories, 1.7g fat, 10.8g carbohydrates, 1.7g fiber, 2.2g sugars, 2.9g protein ·

# Cranberry Sauce

MAKES 2 CUPS | **GF** | **SF** | **MA** | **P** |

*We always had cranberry sauce at Thanksgiving when I was growing up, but it was the gelatin, tubular-looking kind that came from a can. Years later, after I was married and cooking my very first Thanksgiving dinner, I picked up a bag of cranberries. The bag said to boil the cranberries with water and add sugar. I looked at my husband and said, "That's it? That's all you do? Why do people buy it in a can?" Indeed, a real head-scratcher.*

12  oz fresh cranberries
    sweetener (see note)
 1  orange (optional)

1. In a medium saucepan, combine cranberries with 1 cup water; cover and bring to a boil.
2. Once boiling, reduce heat to medium-low and continue to cook for 10–15 minutes, until the cranberries have all popped and it looks like cranberry sauce.
3. Add sweetener to taste (see note), plus a pinch or two of orange zest for a hint of citrus, if desired. Chill for several hours before serving.

▶▶▶ **CHEF'S NOTE:**
*You can use agave nectar, maple syrup, or stevia as your sweetener. When using agave nectar or maple syrup, I tend to add 2 tbsp at the end of cooking, then another 1–2 tbsp to taste once it's chilled. (That's the beauty of those liquid sweeteners; they combine right in—even if it's a cold food—unlike sugar, which only dissolves into hot contents.) If you're using stevia, add it to taste, a very light sprinkle at a time, once the sauce has thoroughly chilled.*

**Per serving (¼ c, without sweetener):** 20 calories, 0.1g fat, 5.2g carbohydrates, 2g fiber, 1.7g sugars, 0.2g protein

# Sweet Potato Casserole

SERVES 4-6 | **GF** | **SF** | **MA** | **P** |

*Sweet potato casserole has been around all my life (it is a favorite of my parents') but I didn't try it until a few years ago. While most recipes call for lots of sugar, I use carrots to make mine naturally sweet (double veggie points!).*

5–6  carrots, chopped
  4  sweet potatoes, cooked and skinned
     cinnamon or pumpkin pie spice, to taste
  2  tbsp cornstarch

**FOR THE CASSEROLE TOPPINGS:**
brown sugar
cornflakes
vegan marshmallows
pecans

1. Fill a large pot with about 2–3 inches water. Bring to a boil and add carrots.
2. Cook until carrots are very tender, about 5–8 minutes. Drain, but reserve liquid.
3. Use electric beaters to whip cooked sweet potato and carrot together, adding carrot cooking water as necessary. (You want a creamy whipped-potatoes consistency.)
4. Add cinnamon or pumpkin pie spice as desired.
5. Preheat oven to 350°F.
6. When potato-carrot mixture is cool, stir in cornstarch.
7. Transfer to a shallow casserole dish. Spread evenly.
8. Top with brown sugar, cornflakes, vegan marshmallows, pecans—or whatever you like.
9. Bake for 30 minutes until thoroughly warm and toppings are toasted.

**Per serving (serving 6, with 5 carrots, no toppings):** 90 calories, 0.2g fat, 20.9g carbohydrates, 4.1g fiber, 7.3g sugars, 2g protein

# Stuffed Acorn Squash

SERVES 2 | **GF** | **SF** | **MA** | **P** |

*This recipe from* Happy Herbivore Abroad *works as an easy, fuss-free (but delicious) meal on Thanksgiving for solo diners or couples!*

    1    acorn squash
    ½    c quinoa
    1¼   c vegetable broth
    ¼    tsp mild curry powder
         about ⅛ tsp ground cinnamon
    ¼    c raisins
    1    c spinach, finely chopped

1. Preheat oven to 400°F.
2. Cut acorn squash in half, place cut side down on a cookie sheet, and bake for 30–35 minutes, until fork-tender.
3. Meanwhile, combine quinoa, vegetable broth, curry powder, a few dashes of cinnamon, and raisins in a pot. Bring to a boil, immediately reduce heat to low, and cook for 15 minutes, or until liquid evaporates. If quinoa is not fluffy after 15 minutes, add more vegetable broth and cook longer. (Sometimes the raisins will absorb the liquid also, so more broth may be needed to cook the quinoa. I find this is particularly true with electric stoves.)
4. After quinoa is done, stir in spinach, add another dash or two of cinnamon, plus salt if desired, then cover and set aside, away from heat.
5. Once acorn squash is done, flip it over and scoop out seeds. Then use a sharp knife to cut the point off each base so the acorn bowls sit upright and don't fall over.
6. Spoon quinoa mixture into squash and serve warm.

**Per serving:** 302 calories, 2.8g fat, 65.8g carbohydrates, 7.2g fiber, 11.4g sugars, 8.4g protein

# Pumpkin Pie

SERVES 9 | **GF\*** | **SF\*** | **MA** | **P** |

*This pie is incredible. It's totally crustless but still firms up like the real deal so you can cut individual slices without it falling apart. It's like a little Thanksgiving tofu miracle.*

    ½    c silken tofu* (see note)
    1½   c nondairy milk
    2    tbsp cornstarch
    1    tsp vanilla extract
    2    c canned pure pumpkin
    ½    c whole-wheat pastry flour* (see note)
    2    tsp baking powder
    ½    c brown sugar
    ¼    tsp fine salt
    3    tsp pumpkin pie spice

1. Preheat oven to 350°F.
2. Set aside a shallow 9-inch glass pie dish.
3. In a blender or food processor, blend tofu, nondairy milk, cornstarch, and vanilla until smooth, stopping to scrape sides periodically.
4. Add remaining ingredients and blend for about a minute more until the mixture is uniform and well combined.
5. Pour the mixture into the pie dish and bake for 1 hour.
6. Allow the pie to cool on the counter, away from the hot oven, until it's at room temperature.
7. Cover with plastic wrap and refrigerate overnight or for at least 4 hours.

▶▶▶ **CHEF'S NOTES:**
- *Mori-Nu extra-firm silken tofu works best in this recipe.*
- *For a soy-free dish, try using ½ cup raw cashews (soaked overnight so they blend well) instead of tofu.*
- *To make this gluten-free, brown rice flour may be substituted for the pastry flour.*

**Per serving:** 77 calories, 0.6g fat, 16.4g carbohydrates, 1.9g fiber, 10.8g sugars, 2.5g protein

# Pumpkin Cheesecake

HOLIDAY
HIT

SERVES 9 | **MA** | **P** |

*If you're looking for a pumpkin pie that even the pickiest relative will devour, this is it. Since this recipe calls for vegan cream cheese and a graham cracker crust, it isn't as wholesome as my other recipes, but I'm okay with making a few nutritional compromises on big holidays.*

| | |
|---|---|
| 1 | 15-oz can pure pumpkin |
| 1 | 8-oz container vegan cream cheese |
| ⅔ | c light brown sugar |
| 1–2 | tbsp pumpkin pie spice |
| 1 | tsp vanilla extract |
| 2 | tbsp cornstarch |
| 1 | graham cracker pie crust (see note) |
| 6 | oz plain soy yogurt or vegan whipped cream (optional) |
| | ground nutmeg or cinnamon for dusting |

1. Preheat oven to 350°F.
2. Combine pumpkin and vegan cream cheese in a blender or food processor. Blend until smooth and creamy, stopping to scrape the sides as necessary.
3. Add sugar, pumpkin pie spice, vanilla, and cornstarch and blend again for 3 minutes, periodically stopping to scrape the sides as necessary.
4. Pour batter into prepared crust and use a spatula to evenly distribute and smooth out the top.
5. Bake for 40–45 minutes, until fully cooked. The pie will rise during baking and should be about ½ inch higher than where it started.
6. Remove from oven and place on counter, away from heat.
7. Allow pie to cool to room temperature, about 2–3 hours. The pie will fall as it cools; do not be alarmed.
8. Cover and chill overnight or for at least 10 hours.
9. Before serving, slice into 9 pieces and add a dollop of soy yogurt or whipped cream to each, if desired.
10. Sprinkle with nutmeg or cinnamon for garnish.

▶▶▶ **CHEF'S NOTES**:
- *If you don't have a strong blender or processor, leave the vegan cream cheese out for 20–30 minutes to soften it up.*
- *Most prepared graham cracker pie crusts are vegan. If you can't find one, or you'd like to make your own to make it a smidgen more healthy, crumble up 2½ cups whole-wheat graham crackers (into the consistency of coarse sand). Add 7–8 tbsp applesauce and stir. Using your fingers, press mixture into a glass pie dish to form a crust. Bake for 8 minutes at 350°F. Allow crust to cool completely before using. Add pie filling and bake normally.*

**Per serving:** 156 calories, 4.6g fat, 27.3 carbohydrates, 1.6g fiber, 16.2g sugars, 1.8g protein

## A GRACIOUS TOUCH

Set name displays by each place setting with the person's name plus a short note why you're thankful for them (let them know they're appreciated!) or why you're thankful in general. To display it nicely, roll up the note and then tie a ribbon around it and leave it on the person's plate. I like finding creative ways to make the day about Thanksgiving–*giving thanks*–instead of "Turkey Day."

# Mini Pumpkin Pies

SERVES 2 | **Q** | **GF** | **SF** | **MA** | **P** |

*This recipe makes two individual servings of pumpkin pie, which, without a crust, is a bit more like pudding or a custard—but still delicious! It's also a great way to use up leftover sweet potato or pumpkin puree. Serve as a snack, treat, or even breakfast. You can also serve these mini pies at dinner parties—just glam it up with garnishes!*

- ⅓ c nondairy milk (see note)
- 2 tsp cornstarch
- ½ c canned pure pumpkin or mashed sweet potato
- 2–3 tbsp brown sugar
- ½ tsp pumpkin pie spice

1. Preheat oven to 350°F.
2. In a small saucepan, whisk nondairy milk with cornstarch until combined. Then whisk in remaining ingredients.
3. Bring to a low boil (just bubbling) until it thickens, about 3–4 minutes.
4. Pour mixture into two small ramekins or other oven-safe dishes.
5. Bake for 25–30 minutes until pies set. (Watch out for cracking, which is usually a sign it's overbaked, and the top will get chewy.)
6. Let cool completely, then refrigerate for at least 3 hours before serving.

▸▸▸ **CHEF'S NOTES:**
- *Bake time will vary if your dishes are larger or smaller.*
- *If you're using sweet potatoes instead of pumpkin, use ½ cup nondairy milk rather than ⅓ cup.*
- *You can halve this recipe for a single serving.*

**Per serving:** 72 calories, 0.6g fat, 16.7 carbohydrates, 2g fiber, 10.8g sugars, 0.9g protein

# Winter Holidays

I find that winter holidays, unlike Thanksgiving, don't have a widely accepted or "traditional" menu. What's served for dinner seems to be different for every family. My family (in case you were wondering) ate fish sticks, crab, and macaroni and cheese on Christmas Eve and lasagna on Christmas Day.

Although I never thought much about it growing up, looking back I have to wonder, who had the wild idea to pair fish with macaroni and cheese? Nevertheless, this tradition has been going on in my family longer than I've been alive, so I doubt it's changing anytime soon! (I've also created my own plant-based dishes that replicate my family's traditional menu [see p. 30] for myself and my parents to enjoy.)

In this section I've included a few options that I think would make for a nice holiday dinner, whatever winter holiday that might be for you!

For Hanukkah ideas see the menu suggestion on pg. 38. For Kwanza, pg. 33. Or try the Nordic experience p. 33.

---

### MENU

**MAIN DISHES**

Portobello Pot Roast (p. 30)
West African Peanut
  Stew (p. 33)
Swedish "Meatballs" (p. 33)
Lasagna (p. 34)

*Another great main dish is*
**Portobello Brisket** *(see variation*
*in Portobello Steaks in Romantic*
*Occasions, p. 86).*

**SIDES**

mashed potatoes (p. 18)
Skillet Green Bean
  Casserole (p. 19)
Brown Gravy (p. 87)

**DRINKS**

"Eggnog" (p. 35)
Hot Toddy (p. 37)
Mulled Cider (p. 37)
Hot Chocolate (p. 37)

**DESSERTS**

Apple Charoset (p. 38)
Cheesecake (p. 38)
Rum Cake (p. 40)
Soft Molasses Cookies (p. 42)
Anise Cookies (p. 42)
Rice Pudding (p. 43)

*If you'd like to include appetizers,*
*I recommend "Cheese" Ball (p. 46)*
*and Baked Mac Bites (p. 52).*

---

# Portobello Pot Roast

HOLIDAY HIT

SERVES 2 | **Q** | **GF**∗ | **SF**∗ |

*When I was flipping through magazines*
*looking for Christmas meal ideas, beef pot*
*roast kept popping up. When I see "beef"*
*my mind immediately thinks "portobello."*
*I like to serve this dish over creamy polenta*
*(see note) or mashed potatoes.*

2   c No-Beef Broth (p. 168), divided∗
1   small onion, sliced thin
3–4 garlic cloves, minced
2–3 carrots, sliced
1   parsnip, sliced (optional)
4   portobello mushrooms, de-stemmed, cut
    into strips
1   c water
2   tbsp balsamic vinegar
6–8 sprigs fresh thyme (intact)
1   sprig fresh rosemary (intact)
    Vegan Worcestershire Sauce (p. 171) (optional)∗

1. Line a large pot with a thin layer of broth. Sauté onion and garlic until onion is translucent.
2. Add carrots and parsnip, if using, plus remaining broth.
3. Add portobello strips on top of carrots and veggies and pour water over top.
4. Drizzle balsamic vinegar over the mushrooms, then add your herbs.
5. Cover, bring to a boil, then reduce heat to low and let simmer until vegetables and mushrooms are very tender, about 20 minutes.
6. Season with salt and pepper and, if desired, add Worcestershire to taste.

▶▶▶ **CHEF'S NOTE:**
*To make polenta, bring 2 cups water to a boil. Reduce*
*heat to low and slowly whisk in 1 cup yellow cornmeal.*
*(It'll clump, so keep stirring—you want smooth!) Add*
*nondairy milk (about ½ cup) as necessary to thin it*
*out (this will also make it creamy).*

**Per serving:** 161 calories, 1.4g fat, 28g carbohydrates, 9.9g fiber, 6.2g
sugars, 13.3g protein

# West African Peanut Stew

HOLIDAY HIT

SERVES 2 | **Q** | **GF** | **SF** | **MA** | **P** |

*This recipe visits from my 7-Day Meal Plan service (getmealplans.com). It's a "cheater" recipe since it uses a bit of peanut butter, but peanuts are a traditional ingredient in many African dishes. Serve as a soup or spoon it over whole-wheat couscous (or quinoa, for a gluten-free option).*

> 1  c vegetable broth, divided
> 1  small onion, diced
> 3–4  garlic cloves, minced
> 1  tbsp fresh minced ginger
> 1  tsp tomato paste
> 1  8-oz can tomato sauce
> 2–3  tbsp peanut butter
> ¼  c canned pure pumpkin
> 8  oz water
> 2  sweet potatoes, diced
>    dash or two of cayenne pepper
>    dash of ground cinnamon
> 2  bay leaves
> 1  tsp ground coriander
>    fresh cilantro, to taste
>    chopped peanuts for garnish (optional)

1. Line a large pot with a thin layer of broth. Sauté onion, garlic, and ginger until onion is translucent.
2. Add tomato paste, remaining broth, tomato sauce, 2 tbsp peanut butter, and pumpkin. Fill tomato sauce can with water and pour in.
3. Add sweet potatoes, a dash or two of cayenne, a light dash of cinnamon, and bay leaves. Cover and bring to a boil.
4. Reduce heat to low and let simmer until potatoes are tender, about 7 minutes.
5. Uncover and scoop out bay leaves. Let soup cool for a few minutes. Stir in coriander.
6. Let cool for a few more minutes and taste, adding more peanut butter, tomato paste, or coriander as desired. Add salt to taste if necessary (the saltiness of peanut butters varies).
7. Stir in fresh cilantro as desired and serve. Garnish with peanuts and a sprig of cilantro on top to be fancy pants!

▶▶▶ **CHEF'S NOTE:**

*For a full Kwanzaa menu, pair with Cornbread (p. 19), mashed sweet potatoes (see "Mashed Potatoes a Dozen Ways," p. 18), Baked Mac Bites (p. 52), Deviled "Eggs" (p. 120), and Creamed Kale (p. 65) or Black-Eyed Pea Collard Greens (p. 61).*

**Per serving (with 2 tbsp peanut butter):** 283 calories, 8.7g fat, 46.4g carbohydrates, 9g fiber, 17.9g sugars, 9.4g protein

# Swedish "Meatballs"

SERVES 2 | **Q** | **GF\*** | **MA** | **P** |

*My husband is part Swedish, so he grew up eating Swedish meatballs during the holidays. (It's a popular Christmas dish in many Nordic countries.) This dish makes for a cozy winter holiday meal as well as a beautiful appetizer or party potluck dish.*

> **FOR THE MEATBALLS:**
> 1  8-oz pkg tempeh, cubed
>    low-sodium soy sauce*
>
> **FOR THE GRAVY:**
> 1  c water
> 1  tbsp low-sodium soy sauce*
> 1  tbsp nutritional yeast
> 2  tbsp Vegan Worcestershire Sauce (p. 171)*
> 1  tsp onion powder
> 1  tsp garlic powder
>    dash of allspice
>    dash of ground nutmeg
> ¼  c nondairy milk
> 3  tbsp white whole-wheat flour*
> 1–3  tsp lingonberry jam (see note)
>    cooked brown rice
>    minced parsley for garnish (optional)

*Swedish "Meatballs" continued...*

1. Bring a pot of water to a boil, then add tempeh plus a splash of soy sauce, and boil for 10 minutes. Drain off water (discard) and set warm tempeh aside.
2. In the same pot, whisk water with soy sauce, nutritional yeast, Worcestershire sauce, onion powder, garlic powder, a light dash of allspice, a slightly heavier dash of nutmeg, nondairy milk, flour, and 1 tsp jam until well combined. Cook over medium heat, whisking regularly until warm and gravy-thick.
3. Taste, adding more jam as desired, plus salt and white pepper as desired.
4. Mix tempeh with gravy until well coated, then serve over a bed of brown rice, garnished with parsley, if desired.

▶▶▶ **CHEF'S NOTES:**
- *Since lingonberry jam is hard to come by in America (you might be able to find it in your local Ikea), I use seedless raspberry jam as a substitute. Red currant jam, strawberry jam, or cranberry sauce may also work.*
- *For the full Nordic experience, serve these meatballs with a potato casserole, Savory Glazed Carrots (p. 123, adding fresh parsley), cabbage cooked in cider, Rice Pudding (p. 43), and glogg (mulled wine; see below)!*
- *The classic ingredients of glogg are red wine, sugar, and spices such as cinnamon, cardamom, ginger, cloves, and orange peels. Spices are combined with the wine and heated for about an hour. Sugar is then added to sweeten it (traditional recipes suggest 1 cup sugar for 1 pint of wine). Additional alcohol such as brandy or vodka is also sometimes added. Serve with raisins and blanched almonds (in the drink) and gingersnap cookies. For a nonalcoholic option, use grape juice.*

**Per serving:** 306 calories. 5.5g fat. 47.1g carbohydrates. 11.4g fiber. 4g sugars. 21.8g protein

# Lasagna

SERVES 4 | **GF\*** | **MA** | **P** |

*Lasagna is perhaps the most beloved Italian dish outside of Italy, and for good reason. It's delicious, relatively easy to prepare, and an all-around crowd-pleaser. Freeze leftovers!*

| | |
|---|---|
| 10 | oz frozen spinach |
| | Tofu Ricotta (see below) |
| 15 | lasagna noodles* |
| 2 | 28-oz jars marinara sauce |
| 1 | c brown or white mushrooms, sliced |

FOR THE TOFU RICOTTA:
| | |
|---|---|
| 1 | lb extra-firm tofu |
| ¼ | c nutritional yeast |
| ½ | tsp yellow or white miso (optional) |
| 1 | tsp fresh lemon juice |
| 1 | tbsp Italian seasoning |
| ¼ | tsp onion powder |
| ¼ | tsp garlic powder |

1. Preheat oven to 350°F.
2. Cook frozen spinach according to package instructions, then press out excess water and set aside.
3. To prepare tofu ricotta, give the tofu a good squeeze, pressing out any excess moisture, then crumble into a mixing bowl using your hands. Add remaining tofu ricotta ingredients and stir with a fork or your hands until well combined. Taste, adding another 1 tbsp nutritional yeast if desired, plus more miso, lemon juice, Italian seasoning, or black pepper to taste.
4. Mix spinach into tofu ricotta and set aside.
5. Cook pasta al dente according to package instructions and immediately rinse with cold water, then pat dry with a clean kitchen towel.
6. Spread a very thin layer of marinara sauce on the bottom of a glass casserole dish.

7. Place 5 noodles side by side, covering the bottom. Spread half of the tofu ricotta mixture on the noodles, then spoon a little marinara on top. Place mushrooms on top of the tofu ricotta layer.
8. Place 5 more noodles side by side on top, and spoon marinara on top. Add remaining tofu ricotta mixture and then add another layer of noodles. Spoon remaining marinara on top of tofu ricotta. (You will likely have leftover marinara.)
9. Bake uncovered for 30–35 minutes, until noodles start to get crisp at the edges.

**Per serving:** 378 calories, 5.1g fat, 76.2g carbohydrates, 13.3g fiber, 16.4g sugars, 16.6g protein

# "Eggnog"

SERVES 1 | **Q** | **GF** | **SF** |

*I featured this recipe in* Happy Herbivore Light & Lean *because it's a healthy version of the quintessential holiday drink—that is something to be merry about!*

¾ c vanilla nondairy milk
1 frozen banana
  dash of ground nutmeg
  dash of ground cloves
¼ tsp ground cinnamon for garnish

1. Combine all ingredients in a blender and blend until smooth.
2. Garnish with ground cinnamon and serve.

**Per serving:** 107 calories, 2g fat, 22.9 carbohydrates, 2.8g fiber, 15.1g sugars, 1.3g protein

Hot Toddy

# Hot Toddy

SERVES 1 | **Q** | **GF** | **SF** | **MA** | **P** |

*A cocktail for the cold and flu season!*

    4   oz water
    1–2 oz Irish whiskey (see note)
        sweetener, to taste (see note)
        lemon, to taste
        cinnamon stick for garnish

1. Heat water. Stir in room-temperature whiskey plus sweetener to taste.
2. Add a squeeze or two of lemon juice and stir.
3. Garnish with a slice of lemon and a cinnamon stick.

▶▶▶ **CHEF'S NOTES:**
- *Rum or brandy can be substituted for whiskey. For a nonalcoholic version, try using a tea base such as Earl Grey.*
- *Sugar or honey is traditionally used as a sweetener.*

**Per serving (1 oz whiskey, unsweetened):** 71 calories, 0g fat, 0.1g carbohydrates, 0g fiber, 0g sugars, 0g protein

# Mulled Cider

MAKES 8 CUPS | **Q** | **GF** | **SF** | **MA** | **P** |

*My sister Courtney taught me how to make this slow-cooked cider in a coffee pot. It's so simple!*

    ½   tsp whole allspice
    1   tsp whole cloves
    1–2 cinnamon sticks
        pinch of ground nutmeg
    1   orange, quartered
        brown sugar, to taste (optional)
    ½   gallon apple cider

1. Place coffee filter in basket of coffeepot.
2. Add whole seasonings, nutmeg, orange pieces, and sugar (if using) into the filter.
3. Pour cider into where water usually goes.
4. Brew and serve.

▶▶▶ **CHEF'S NOTE:**
*For an "adult" drink, add rum to individual servings.*

**Per serving (1 cup):** 117 calories, 0.3g fat, 29g carbohydrates, 0g fiber, 27g sugars, 0.1g protein

# Hot Chocolate

SERVES 1 | **Q** | **GF** | **SF** | **MA** | **P** |

*You're less than five minutes away from hot chocolate... get to it!*

    1   c nondairy milk
    1   tbsp agave nectar
    1   tbsp unsweetened cocoa
    1   tsp vegan chocolate chips
        dash or two of ground cinnamon

1. Combine all ingredients in a blender and whiz until smooth.
2. Gently heat over low in a pan on the stovetop or in the microwave using the beverage setting.

▶▶▶ **CHEF'S NOTE:**
*If you have a Blendtec or Vitamix, you can place all ingredients in the blender and let it run for 3 minutes or until it's hot.*

**Per serving (with chocolate chips):** 128 calories, 4.4g fat, 23.9g carbohydrates, 2.8g fiber, 18.7g sugars, 2.3g protein

# Apple Charoset

SERVES 4 | **Q** | **GF** | **SF** |

*I find the exact ratio of these ingredients varies by individual tastes and family traditions, but the core ingredients for a charoset are apples, nuts, sweet wine, honey (or agave nectar for vegans), and cinnamon. Some recipes call for raisins or dates (which I use in lieu of nuts for a low-fat version), and others have lemon or orange flavors added. Basically, it's a flexible recipe open to your tastes!*

|   |   |
|---|---|
| 3 | c peeled and shredded apples (see note) |
| ¾ | c chopped almonds or walnuts (optional) (see note) |
| ¼ | c raisins or chopped dates (optional) (see note) |
| 3–4 | tbsp sweet wine (e.g., Manischewitz) |
| 1 | tbsp honey or agave nectar |
| ¼ | tsp ground cinnamon |
|   | lemon zest (optional) and juice |

1. Mix apples with nuts and/or raisins, then mix in 3 tbsp wine, honey or agave nectar, and cinnamon, stirring to combine.
2. Add a pinch of lemon zest if desired, plus juice of ¼–½ lemon, and mix again.
3. Taste, adding more honey, lemon, wine, or cinnamon as desired.
4. Refrigerate for at least 30 minutes, but preferably 2 hours. (Don't make too far ahead or it may get brown and watery.)

▶▶▶ **CHEF'S NOTES:**
- *I like Fuji, Granny Smith, and Gala apples (or a combination) best.*
- *You can use both nuts and raisins or dates, or you can omit one or the other.*
- *For a more intense flavor, soak raisins or dates in wine.*
- *For a complete Hanukkah menu, pair with Portobello Brisket (p. 86), Beet Salad (p. 120), Sweet*

*Potato Casserole (p. 23; make it savory by adding cumin and omitting the sweet stuff!), plus Mark's Baked Vegan Latkes recipe shared on happyherbivore.com! Soft Pretzels (p. 159) and Chocolate Glazed Doughnuts (on happyherbivore.com) are fun options, too!*

**Per serving:** 181 calories, 8.8g fat, 22.6g carbohydrates, 4.5g fiber, 14.6g sugars, 4.1g protein

# Cheesecake

SERVES 9 | **MA** | **P** |

*Vegan cheesecake became a Christmas tradition in my family after my parents went plant-based. What's funny is we never really ate cheesecake before (or had any kind of Christmas dessert tradition), but that's part of the fun in the plant-based journey. My parents, and even our very skeptical, very omni relatives, devour this cheesecake. Like the Pumpkin Cheesecake (p. 26), this recipe is more decadent than my other recipes and uses ingredients I normally wouldn't . . . except during the holidays!*

|   |   |
|---|---|
| 1 | 12.3-oz pkg Mori-Nu tofu (see note) |
| 1 | 8-oz container vegan cream cheese |
| ⅔ | c raw sugar |
| ¾ | tsp almond extract |
| 2 | tbsp cornstarch |
|   | graham cracker pie crust (see note) |
|   | frozen strawberries for topping |

*Cheesecake continued...*

1. Preheat oven to 350°F.
2. Drain tofu and transfer to a blender along with cream cheese.
3. Blend for 30 seconds, scrape the sides, and blend for 30 seconds more.
4. Add remaining ingredients except crust and strawberries and blend for 3 minutes, scraping the sides periodically.
5. Pour batter into prepared crust and use a spatula to evenly distribute and smooth out the top.
6. Bake for 40–45 minutes and then place on the counter away from the hot oven to cool to room temperature.
7. Chill overnight in the fridge or for at least 10 hours.
8. For a topping, let frozen strawberries defrost (in a bowl or in their bag). Serve over the cheesecake.

>>> **CHEF'S NOTES:**

- *If you don't have a strong blender or processor, leave the vegan cream cheese out for 20–30 minutes to soften it up.*
- *Any Mori-Nu tofu will do here, but extra-firm is best.*
- *Most prepared graham cracker pie crusts are vegan. If you can't find one, or you'd like to make your own to make it a smidgen more healthy, crumble up 2½ cups whole-wheat graham crackers (into the consistency of coarse sand). Add 7–8 tbsp applesauce and stir. Using your fingers, press mixture into a glass pie dish to form a crust. Bake for 8 minutes at 350°F. Allow crust to cool completely before using. Add pie filling and bake normally.*

**Per serving (without crust):** 158 calories, 7.5g fat, 18.8g carbohydrates, 0g fiber, 16.8g sugars, 5.7g protein

# Rum Cake

SERVES 9 | **SF** | **MA** | **P** |

*I try not to play favorites with my recipes, but this recipe from* Everyday Happy Herbivore *is in my all-time top five favorites, and it's a terrific dish for celebrating Christmas or any other winter holiday.*

**FOR THE CAKE:**
1 c oat flour (p. 42; see note)
1 c white whole-wheat flour
1 tsp baking powder
½ tsp baking soda
½ tsp fine salt
1 tsp ground cinnamon
⅔ c light brown sugar
¼ c molasses (*not* blackstrap)
¼ c unsweetened applesauce
1 tsp vanilla extract
½ c dark rum
½ c nondairy milk

**FOR THE ICING:**
1 c powdered sugar
1 tsp dark rum
1 tbsp tangerine or orange zest
2 tsp nondairy milk

1. Preheat oven to 350°F.
2. Set aside a 8- or 9-inch nonstick square pan or a nonstick Bundt pan.
3. In a medium-size mixing bowl, combine flours, baking powder, baking soda, salt, cinnamon, and sugar.
4. Add wet ingredients in order, then stir to combine.
5. Pour into prepared pan and bake for 25–40 minutes, until a toothpick inserted in the middle comes out clean. (Usually it takes about 35 minutes, but can vary based on pan size and type.)
6. Meanwhile, make icing. In a small bowl, whisk powdered sugar with rum and zest;

*Rum Cake continued…*

whisk in nondairy milk a little at a time, until a runny glaze forms.

7. Spoon the icing over the warm cake and let it run down the sides.

▶▶▶ **CHEF'S NOTES:**

- *To make oat flour, whiz 1 cup instant oats or 1 cup plus 2 tbsp rolled oats in your blender until it reaches a flour-like consistency.*
- *The tangerine zest really takes this cake to a whole new level of delicious awesomeness!*

**Per serving (with icing):** 244 calories, 1.2g fat, 49.2g carbohydrates, 2.6g fiber, 30.6g sugars, 3.7g protein
**Per serving (without icing):** 190 calories, 1.2g fat, 35.7g carbohydrates, 2.6g fiber, 17.4g sugars, 3.6g protein
**Per serving of icing (1 tbsp):** 61 calories, 0g fat, 15.2g carbohydrates, 0g fiber, 14.9g sugars, 0.1g protein

# Soft Molasses Cookies

MAKES 14 | **Q** | **GF** | **SF** | **MA** | **P** |

*I take these soft and fluffy cookies to all my holiday potlucks—they're always a hit!*

| | |
|---|---|
| 1 | c oat flour (p. 42; see note) |
| 1 | tbsp cornstarch |
| ½–1 | tsp baking soda (see note) |
| | pinch of fine salt |
| ½ | tsp ground cinnamon |
| ¼ | tsp ground ginger |
| ⅛ | tsp allspice, ground nutmeg, or ground cloves |
| ¼ | c mashed navy beans |
| ¼ | c molasses (*not* blackstrap) |
| 2 | tbsp unsweetened applesauce |
| 2 | tbsp brown or raw sugar (optional) |

1. Mix oat flour, cornstarch, baking soda, salt, and spices together in a mixing bowl until well combined.
2. Add remaining ingredients and stir until just combined.
3. Set batter aside to rest while oven heats to 350°F.

4. Line a cookie sheet with parchment paper.
5. Drop 14 spoonfuls of batter onto the cookie sheet.
6. Bake for 10–15 minutes or until cookies are firm to the touch.

▶▶▶ **CHEF'S NOTE:**

*For a less puffy and denser cookie, use only ½ tsp of baking soda. Use the full teaspoon for very soft and pillow-like cookies.*

**Per cookie:** 47 calories, 0.7g fat, 9.9g carbohydrates, 0.8g fiber, 3.5g sugars, 0.9g protein

# Anise Cookies

MAKES 8 | **Q** | **GF** | **SF** | **MA** | **P** |

*I grew up eating Italian anise cookies every year at Christmas. After seeing them again when I was in Italy (researching recipes for* Happy Herbivore Abroad*), I came home and finally adapted my grandmother's recipe. If you're unfamiliar with anise, it tastes a lot like black licorice.*

**FOR THE COOKIES:**

| | |
|---|---|
| 1 | c oat flour (p. 42; see note) |
| 1 | tbsp cornstarch |
| ½ | tsp baking soda |
| | pinch of fine salt |
| ¼ | c white beans, mashed (see note) |
| ½ | tsp anise extract |
| ¼ | c pure maple syrup |
| ¼ | c unsweetened applesauce |
| 1–2 | tbsp raw sugar (optional) |
| | splash of nondairy milk (optional) |

**FOR THE ICING:**

| | |
|---|---|
| 1 | c powdered sugar |
| 5 | tsp nondairy milk |
| | anise extract, to taste |

1. Preheat oven to 350°F. Line a cookie sheet with parchment paper and set aside.

2. Whisk flour with cornstarch, baking soda, and a pinch of salt until combined.

3. Add beans, anise extract, maple syrup, apple-sauce, and sugar, if using. Stir to combine—it might look dry at first, but keep combining. If dryness persists, add a splash of nondairy milk (when in doubt, wetter is better).

4. Flour your hands and pick off 8 walnut-sized pieces of dough. Roll each into a ball, then flat-ten into mini "hockey puck" shapes.

5. Bake for 10–14 minutes or until golden and firm to the touch (the cookies will puff up).

6. Meanwhile, prepare icing by combining powdered sugar and 5 tsp nondairy milk to form a thick paste, adding anise extract one drop at a time. (A little bit goes a long, long way!)

7. Once cookies are done baking, allow to cool, then slather icing on top before serving.

▶▶▶ **CHEF'S NOTES:**
- *White whole-wheat or whole-wheat pastry flour may be substituted for the oat flour.*
- *My grandmother also added a little colored sprin-kle balls to her cookies.*
- *Any white bean, such as cannellini, navy, or butter beans (cooked or canned), may be used in this recipe.*

Per cookie: 90 calories, 0.3g fat, 20.2g carbohydrates, 2.1g fiber, 7.1g sugars, 2.5g protein

# Rice Pudding

SERVES 2 | **GF** | **SF** | **MA** | **P** |

*Rich and creamy, this rice pudding is just as good for you as it is delicious! Although rice pudding is a common winter holiday dessert, I actually love it most during the hot summer. Cold rice pudding is better than ice cream, I swear! (And no hot oven required!)*

⅓ c brown rice, uncooked
2 c nondairy milk, divided
2 tbsp cornstarch
⅓ c raisins
  sweetener, to taste (optional)
  dash of ground cinnamon
  pure maple syrup, for drizzling (optional)

1. Combine rice with 1 cup nondairy milk in a saucepan, cover, and bring to a boil over high heat. Once boiling, reduce to low and continue to cook until rice is cooked and all the nondairy milk has been absorbed.

2. Meanwhile, whisk remaining nondairy milk with cornstarch until well combined.

3. Once rice is cooked, stir in milk/cornstarch mixture and raisins. Bring to a boil over high heat and reduce to medium once boiling. Allow the pudding to thicken up, stirring occasionally. Add sweetener here if desired (for example, brown sugar, agave, or pure maple syrup—I find the raisins make it sweet enough, especially with sweetened nondairy milk, but most traditional recipes call for sugar). If the pudding becomes too thick, thin out with more nondairy milk. If it's not thick enough, continue to cook.

4. Once thick and creamy (about 3–5 minutes) stir in cinnamon as desired (I like ¼–½ tsp).

5. Allow pudding to completely cool, then trans-fer to fridge in an airtight container. Chill for several hours before serving. Drizzle a little maple syrup over top to sweeten it more before serving, if desired.

Per serving: 248 calories, 3.5g fat, 51.7g carbohydrates, 3.1g fiber, 14.3g sugars, 4.1g protein

# New Year's Eve

Compared to my other parties during the year, my New Year's Eve bash is always a touch more elegant. Maybe it's the champagne, the emotion of closing another year, or the simple fact that my friends show up in dresses and ties rather than jeans and football jerseys.

Whatever the explanation, I want my NYE party to feel mature, *sophisticated*. That means 7-Layer Dip (while tasty) need not apply. A variety of finger food appetizers is the way to go. Glam up your favorite party foods by making them single-serving. (Think meatballs on toothpicks.)

It's amazing how much fancier pudding feels in a shot glass! Or cheesy mashed potatoes (see "Mashed Potatoes a Dozen Ways," p. 18) in a small bowl with a garnish of smoked paprika. Even the 7-Layer Dip I just pooh-poohed feels more stylish and upscale when you offer single servings in a cup. **Think bite-size.** Serve small portions that are irresistibly easy for your guests to pop into their mouths. Get creative, too! If you love something, find a way to break it down into a single (plant-based) serving. For example, a few years ago I made vegan BLT skewers instead of sandwiches. Small piece of toast, lettuce, a cherry tomato, piece of tempeh bacon (repeat)—voilà! They went so fast! Fruit kabobs (p. 133) are always popular, too!

## MENU

### DIPS, SPREADS & TOPPERS

"Cheese" Ball (p. 46)
Spinach & Artichoke Dip (p. 46)
No-Eggplant Caponata (p. 48)
Bruschetta & Crostini (p. 49)

### SMALL BITES

Cajun Stuffed Mushrooms (p. 50)
"Tuna" Salad (p. 50)

Spring Rolls (p. 52)
Cowboy Caviar (p. 54)

### BIGGER BITES

Meatloaf Bites (p. 51)
Baked Mac Bites (p. 52)
Artisan Pizza (see Whole-
    Wheat Pizza Dough, p. 169)
Crab Cakes with
    Rémoulade Sauce (p. 53)

### DRINK

Champagne with a frozen
    fruit dropped in

*Additional menu items ideal
for New Year's Eve are Southern
Caviar (p. 60), Deviled "Eggs"
(p. 120), Lemon-Rosemary
Meatballs (p. 127), and Mini
Soy-Free Quiche (p. 128), found
in later Occasion sections.*

# "Cheese" Ball

HOLIDAY HIT

MAKES 1 BALL | **Q** | **GF** | **MA** | **P** |

*I was never much of a cheese fanatic, but
oh how I loved cheese balls at Christmas.
I love this healthier "cheese" ball even
more and I make it anytime I'm having
company over or going to a party. It never
lasts more than a few minutes!*

- ½  c cooked chickpeas
- ⅓  block of extra-firm tofu (about 5 oz)
- 5  tbsp nutritional yeast
- 1  tbsp yellow miso
     few drops of liquid smoke
     few drops of agave nectar
- 1  tsp prepared yellow mustard
- ½  tsp onion powder
- ½  tsp garlic powder
     smoked paprika for garnish (optional)
     almond slices for garnish (optional)

1. Combine all ingredients except garnishes in a
   food processor until smooth and paste-like.
2. Spoon mixture out into a metal bowl, then
   use a rubber spatula to scrape and smooth it
   into a ball.
3. Cover with plastic wrap and chill for a few hours.

4. Transfer to your serving plate and garnish
   with smoked paprika and almond slices on the
   outside, if desired.

**Per serving (1 tsp):** 30 calories, 0.7g fat, 3.7g carbohydrates, 1.3g
fiber, 0.5g sugars, 2.8g protein

# Spinach & Artichoke Dip

SERVES 4 | **Q** | **GF** | **SF** | **MA** | **PA** | **P** |

*Spinach and artichoke dip that's good for
you? It's possible! Spread this dip on crusty
whole-grain bread or serve with crackers,
raw vegetables, and/or whole-wheat pita
warmed and cut into triangles.*

- 12  oz frozen spinach
- 4-8  garlic cloves, minced
- 1  small onion, diced
- ¼  c vegetable broth or spinach water
- 1  c cooked white beans (see note)
- ½  c nondairy milk
- ½  c nutritional yeast
- 1-2  tsp Dijon mustard
- 1  14-oz can artichoke hearts (in water, not
     oil), drained
     AJ's Vegan Parmesan (p. 172) (optional)
     smoked paprika for garnish (optional)

"Cheese" Ball

*Spinach & Artichoke Dip continued . . .*

1. Preheat oven to 350°F. Grab an 8-inch glass pie or casserole dish and set aside.
2. Cook spinach according to package instructions, taking care to press out all the excess water, and set spinach aside.
3. In a small pot or skillet, sauté garlic and onion with ¼ cup vegetable broth over high heat until garlic is golden, onion is translucent, and most of the liquid has evaporated.
4. Transfer onion-garlic mixture to a food processor or blender with beans and nondairy milk. Whiz until smooth and creamy. Add nutritional yeast and Dijon (use less if your brand is spicy or strong), plus salt and pepper, if desired, and blend again.
5. If your artichoke hearts are big, quarter or chop them.
6. Transfer spinach, bean mixture, and artichoke hearts back to the small pot or skillet, mixing to combine. STOP
7. Pour into baking dish and spread out in an even layer. Bake for 10–20 minutes or until warm and the top is golden. Generously garnish with vegan Parmesan and a few light dashes of smoked paprika if using.

▶▶▶ **CHEF'S NOTES**:
- *This dip is for garlic lovers: Add as much garlic as you like. If you don't love garlic, you can scale it back, but I recommend at least 2 good-sized cloves.*
- *Any white beans, such as navy, cannellini, or butter beans, will work in this recipe.*

**Per serving:** 195 calories, 2g fat, 30.2g carbohydrates, 12.9g fiber, 1.2g sugars, 17g protein

**VARIATION**

**Spinach & Artichoke Lasagna:** *My friend Kelly Doughty makes a killer lasagna with this dip. She says, "I double the recipe, thin it out with an additional cup of nondairy milk at the time of blending, build the lasagna normally, and top with vegan Parm."*

# No-Eggplant Caponata

SERVES 4 | **Q** | **GF** | **SF** | **MA** | **P** |

*I don't "do" eggplant (we all have our preferences, right?), but I love the idea of caponata. With this cookbook I decided to try my hand at an eggplant-free version and I'm hopelessly in love. This caponata fits any party, from brunch to Super Bowl Sunday to something a little more fancy like a wine party or New Year's Eve. I've also tossed leftovers with pasta for a quick meal and eaten it by itself for a light summer lunch.*

¼   c raisins
    vegetable broth, as needed
2   red bell peppers, seeded and diced
1   small onion, diced small
2   garlic cloves, minced
    red pepper flakes
1   tomato, diced (see note)
¼   c minced green olives (5–10 olives)
3   tbsp capers
2   bay leaves
    red wine vinegar, to taste (optional)
    fresh basil, chiffonade

1. Soak raisins in hot water for 10 minutes. (Water from the tap is usually not hot enough, but water heated on the stove to an almost boil, or water heated via the beverage setting on your microwave, is hot enough.)
2. Meanwhile, line a skillet with a thin layer of broth and sauté bell peppers, onion, garlic, and a dash or two of red pepper flakes until onion is translucent and broth has evaporated.
3. Add tomato with juices, green olives, capers, bay leaves, soaked raisins, plus raisin water as necessary to prevent sticking or burning.

Continue to cook until bell peppers are very tender.

4. Remove bay leaves and let rest so flavors can meld.

5. Season with salt and pepper if desired. You can also add red wine vinegar to taste if desired. If it's too tart, add a little sweetener such as sugar or a drop of agave.

6. Stir in basil just before serving. Serve on crusty bread or crackers.

▶▶▶ **CHEF'S NOTES:**
- *You can sub ¼ cup canned tomatoes for the tomato.*
- *To chiffonade, cut your basil into long, thin strips.*

**Per serving (with 10 olives):** 73 calories, 1.5g fat, 14.7g carbohydrates, 2.7g fiber, 9.1g sugars, 1.6g protein

# B R U S C H E T T A  &  C R O S T I N I

Let's be honest: "bruschetta" and "crostini" are just fancier names for toast (but I'm fancy pants!). Either one is an easy (and beautiful) option for a dinner or party appetizer, or for brunch.

## Bruschetta

Traditionally, bruschetta is made with parboiled tomatoes, garlic, fresh basil, olive oil, and (some-

times) balsamic vinegar. Taking a trick from the Tostada con Tomate recipe in *Happy Herbivore Abroad*, I like to rub fresh garlic on my bread, toast it, then top it with plum tomatoes (seeded and diced) that I've sautéed in a little broth with fresh garlic, then mixed with chopped fresh basil, balsamic vinegar (optional), and a splash of brine from the olives or caper jar (to replace the taste of olive oil), plus salt and black pepper. Capers or olives, as well as lemon juice, add a nice twist to the classic bruschetta recipe.

## Crostini

Crostini means "little toasts" in Italian, but you don't have to use Italian bread to make crostini. Any crusty bread or plain ol' toast served with a savory topping and garnish can pass for crostini. White Bean Dill Dip (p. 118), Olive Tapenade (p. 89), and No-Eggplant Caponata (p. 48) are some of my party favorites, but I've also gone a simpler route with hummus or guacamole.

▶▶▶ **CHEF'S NOTE:**
*Crusty bread (e.g., Italian bread or a baguette) roasted in the oven (about 5 minutes at 350°F) or on the grill in the summer works the best. My local bakery makes no-oil, vegan, whole-wheat bread for me by request; just ask, yours might, too!*

# Cajun Stuffed Mushrooms

MAKES 12 | **Q** | **GF** | **SF** | **MA** | **PA** | **P** |

*These mushrooms, inspired by a Weight Watchers recipe my colleagues used to bring to holiday parties, will dazzle anyone they're served to—they're my go-to party app all year long!*

    vegetable broth, divided
¼   c red bell pepper, finely diced
¼   c celery, finely diced
¼   c onion, finely diced
4   garlic cloves, minced
1   tsp Cajun Seasoning (p. 173)
    hot sauce (optional)
1   c spinach, finely diced
14  oz white mushrooms, de-stemmed

1. Preheat oven to 350°F.
2. Line a large skillet with a thin layer of broth. Add bell pepper, celery, onion, and garlic, and sauté over high heat until bell peppers are soft and onion is translucent, about 2–3 minutes.
3. Stir in Cajun seasoning, adding hot sauce to taste if using.
4. Add spinach and a splash of broth if necessary to prevent sticking, and stir. Continue stirring until spinach is darker green and soft, about a minute or less. Turn off heat and set aside.
5. Place mushrooms bottoms up in a nonstick muffin tin or on a silicone mat.
6. Stuff each mushroom with the spinach filling.
   **STOP**
7. Bake for 10–15 minutes, until mushrooms are tender but not so cooked that they are mushy or falling apart. Serve warm.

Per mushroom: 12 calories, 0.1g fat, 2g carbohydrates, 0.5g fiber, 0.8g sugars, 1.2g protein

# "Tuna" Salad

MAKES 4 | **Q** | **GF\*** | **SF\*** | **MA** | **P** |

*I love serving this as a spreadable dip with crackers or tea sandwich-style for my fancy pants parties and ladies' lunches. It's amazing how chickpeas and a little kelp re-create the taste of tuna!*

1    15-oz can chickpeas, drained and rinsed
2    celery stalks, washed
1–2  tbsp dill pickle relish
½    tsp onion flakes
2    tsp nutritional yeast
1    tbsp low-sodium soy sauce*
3    tbsp Vegan Mayo (p. 170)*
½    tsp kelp granules (see note)
½    tsp fresh lemon juice (optional)

1. In a large mixing bowl, mash chickpeas with a fork until coarse and no whole beans are left. Alternatively, pulse beans in a food processor a few times, being careful not to puree, and transfer to a mixing bowl.
2. Shred celery with a cheese grater or mince in food processor by letting the motor run, but be careful not to pulverize.
3. Transfer to the mixing bowl and add remaining ingredients, stirring to combine. Add more mayo or kelp as necessary or desired.

▶▶▶ **CHEF'S NOTES:**
- *Kelp is a seaweed. You can buy kelp granules at most health food stores (check the "Asian" aisle) or online. A popular brand is Maine Coast Sea Vegetables. It's sold in a small canister, like the kind Parmesan cheese comes in.*
- *For ways to make this into a sandwich, see "Pinwheels & Sandwiches," (p. 141).*

Per serving (without bread): 125 calories, 0.9g fat, 22.6g carbohydrates, 4.4g fiber, 3g sugars, 7.1g protein

# Meatloaf Bites

HOLIDAY
HIT

MAKES 8 | **Q** | **GF** | **SF\*** | **MA** | **P** |

*This recipe from* Happy Herbivore Light & Lean *was an instant hit with my fans, particularly my tiniest ones. Kids just love these mini meatloaves! Top with mashed potatoes and you have a dazzling, savory cupcake. Or just doodle a pretty spiral with ketchup—that's still fancy pants!*

- 1   15-oz can kidney beans, drained and rinsed
- 1   tbsp onion powder
- 1   tbsp garlic powder
- ½–1   tbsp Italian seasoning
- 1   tbsp chili powder (add another 1 tsp if you like it spicy)
- 3   tbsp ketchup
- 2   tbsp mustard
- 1   tbsp Vegan Worcestershire Sauce (p. 171) (optional)*
- 1   c frozen mixed vegetables, thawed
- 6   tbsp instant oats

1. Preheat oven to 350°F.
2. Line a muffin tin with paper liners or use a nonstick pan.
3. Mash beans in a bowl with fork or potato masher until well mashed. Add remaining ingredients, except oats, and stir to combine. Stir in oats.
4. Spoon into muffin tin and pack down. Bake for 20 minutes until crisp on the outside and fairly firm to the touch (firms a bit as it cools). Serve with ketchup, Brown Gravy (p. 87), etc.

**Per bite:** 101 calories, 1.7g fat, 16.9g carbohydrates, 6.5g fiber, 3g sugars, 5.8g protein

# Spring Rolls

SERVES 12 | **Q** | **GF** | **MA** | **P** |

*I'm a glutton for spring rolls in my everyday
life, but they're also great for parties and
potlucks, especially if you have a lot of other
heavy food. Spring rolls are a pop-in-your-
mouth palate cleanser (and portable salad!).
I also love having my friends over for DIY
sushi and spring roll parties (way cheaper
than ordering them out)—and, as a bonus,
kids like to make 'em, too!*

½  lb firm tofu
12  spring roll wrappers
1  carrot, julienned
½  cucumber, julienned
1  c bean sprouts
1½  c lettuce, chopped
1½  c cooked brown rice
    dipping sauce, to taste (see note)

1. Press tofu, then cut the block into 4 slabs. Cut
   each slab into 3 pieces (for a total of 12 sticks)
   and set aside.

2. Use a deep dish, large pot, or baking pan
   that's big enough to easily lay your spring roll
   wrapper in and fill with about ¼ inch water—
   enough water to completely submerge 1
   wrapper. Place 1 spring roll wrapper in the
   water for 30–40 seconds (or according to
   package directions). If the wrapper hasn't
   soaked long enough, it is difficult to wrap; if
   it has soaked for too long, it can easily tear.
   Gently take the soaked wrapper out of the
   water and let excess water gently drip off.

3. Place the wrapper on a flat surface, such as a
   clean cutting board. Place 1 stick of tofu and a
   few pieces of carrot, cucumber, sprouts, and a
   little lettuce and brown rice in the center. Pick
   up the bottom of wrapper and fold it over the
   fillings. Then pick up one side and fold it over,

repeating with the other side. Continue to roll
the wrapper all the way to the top.

4. Set spring roll aside on a dry dish or platter
   and repeat the process with remaining wrappers and fillings.

5. Serve with a dipping sauce.

▶▶▶ **CHEF'S NOTES:**

- *For a dipping sauce, use teriyaki sauce, sweet chili
  sauce, Thai Kitchen Spicy Thai Mango Sauce, or a
  peanut sauce.*
- *My sister Courtney told me her sushi wrap and roll
  trick: Place the wrapper on a cutting board with
  the bottom hanging off of the board. This makes it
  easier to pick the wrapper up and roll it.*

**Per roll (without dipping sauce):** 143 calories, 1.6g fat, 26.2g
carbohydrates, 1.5g fiber, 0.8g sugars, 6.2g protein

# Baked Mac Bites

MAKES 24 OR MORE | **GF\*** | **MA** | **P** |

*Here I've turned my classic mac 'n' cheese
into a "bite" for a fun appetizer! (Make
sure to use small, shell-shaped pasta.)*

½  lb uncooked pasta\*
1¼  c nondairy milk
½  c nutritional yeast
1  tsp prepared yellow mustard
1  tbsp onion flakes
1  tsp garlic powder
½  tsp paprika
¼  tsp turmeric
1  12.3-oz pkg firm Mori-Nu tofu, drained
2  tbsp yellow miso
   bread crumbs (optional)\*
   AJ's Vegan Parmesan (p. 172; optional)
   smoked paprika for garnish

1. Preheat oven to 400°F.

2. Cook pasta al dente according to package directions and immediately rinse with cold water.

3. In a medium saucepan, whisk nondairy
   milk, nutritional yeast, mustard, and spices

together and bring to a boil over medium-high heat.

4. Meanwhile, combine tofu with 2 tbsp water or vegetable broth in a blender. Puree until smooth and set aside.

5. Once the milk mixture is boiling, remove from heat and stir in miso. Then add in cooked pasta and pureed tofu, stirring to coat evenly.

6. Add salt and pepper to taste and stir again.

7. Transfer mixture to a metal muffin tin, filling each cup completely (see note).

8. Top each bite with bread crumbs or vegan Parmesan, if desired, and bake for 15 minutes, or until the tops are slightly browned.

9. Garnish with smoked paprika.

---

▶▶▶ **CHEF'S NOTES:**

• *Some of my testers found they needed to grease their pans, even when using nonstick, if they wanted to pop the bites out while they were still hot or warm. (Spritz with cooking spray or add a drop of oil to a clean paper towel and rub it around in every cup lightly.) I have had luck using a thin plastic knife around the edges of any nonstick pan to get them out warm without using oil. (The bites will pop out for you without grease if they've cooled, but if you don't want cool or room-temp bites, you might need a little slip-and-slide action to get them out while warm.) Everyone had issues with this dish sticking too much to silicone, so use your metal baking pan here.*

• *You can garnish with tempeh bacon bits or sliced chives to be extra fancy pants at a party.*

• *You can make just regular mac 'n' cheese with this recipe by using a big casserole dish and baking longer (20–25 minutes at 350°F).*

**Per serving (43g):** 63 calories, 1.2g fat, 9.6g carbohydrates, 1.5g fiber, 0.5g sugars, 4.2g protein

# Crab Cakes with Rémoulade Sauce

MAKES 5 | **GF\*** | **PA** |

*I tend to serve these crab cakes at my fancier parties (there's just something elegant about a crab cake) and in the summer, when I want a lighter, seafood-like menu. Meanwhile, my friend Natala gets super fancy pants and stuffs this "crab" mixture into mushrooms before baking, for crab-stuffed mushrooms. (They're amazing!)*

CRAB CAKES
- 1 lb extra-firm tofu
- 3 celery stalks, shredded or minced
- 1¼ c oyster mushrooms, coarsely chopped
- ¼ c Vegan Mayo (p. 170)
- 1 tsp onion powder
- ½ tsp garlic powder
- ¾ c instant oats
- 1 tsp kelp granules
- 1 tbsp low-sodium soy sauce\*
- 1 tbsp Old Bay seasoning
- ¼ tsp black pepper
  juice of 1–2 lemon wedges

RÉMOULADE SAUCE:
- 1 tbsp Vegan Mayo (p. 170)
- 1 tbsp plus ¼ tsp ketchup
- 1 tbsp dill relish
- ¼ tsp prepared yellow mustard
  juice of 1 lemon wedge
- ¼ tsp Old Bay seasoning, more as needed
  a few drops hot sauce, to taste

1. Press the tofu for 20 minutes. Shred tofu using a cheese grater or the shredding blade on a food processor. Transfer to a large mixing bowl.

2. Combine remaining ingredients through pepper using your hands. Mix for a few minutes, particularly if you shredded the tofu with a cheese grater, so the strands break down. You want the mixture to be very crumbly, almost like cottage cheese.

*Crab Cakes with Rémoulade Sauce continued...*

3. Set aside and let rest while oven preheats to 350°F. Line a cookie sheet with parchment paper.

4. Taste, adding more Old Bay or kelp if desired to get a fishier or spicier taste. **STOP**

5. Pack a wide ½-cup measuring cup with a portion of the mixture, then transfer molded cake to the prepared cookie sheet. Repeat until you have 5 cakes. If you don't have a wide measuring cup, just use your palm to lightly smash down the patty and shape into a round crab cake.

6. Squeeze the juice from a lemon wedge or two over the patties before baking.

7. Bake for 25–35 minutes, until outside is golden brown and crisp.

8. Make rémoulade by mixing all ingredients together. Add more Old Bay seasoning or hot sauce as desired. Chill until serving. Lightly smear rémoulade on each cake.

**Per crab cake (without sauce):** 78 calories, 1.3g fat, 7.7g carbohydrates, 1g fiber, 2.1g sugars, 8.8g protein

# Cowboy Caviar

SERVES 4 | **Q** | **GF** | **SF** | **MA** |

*A copycat of Trader Joe's Cowboy Caviar (but less sweet), this dump-and-go salsa is amazing warm or cold. Serve it at your next potluck or party.*

- 1  14.5-oz can fire-roasted diced tomatoes, undrained
- 1  15-oz can black beans, drained and rinsed
- 1  16-oz jar salsa verde
- 6  oz frozen corn (see note)
   chili powder, to taste
   chipotle powder, to taste (optional)
   juice of 1 lime (optional)

1. Combine tomatoes (with juices), black beans, salsa, and corn in a large pot or slow cooker. Add several dashes of chili powder (or chipotle if you like it HOT, but remember a little goes a long way!).

2. Taste, adding more spice if desired.

3. Heat over low until thoroughly warm. Add lime juice to taste, if desired, just before serving.

4. Serve warm or cold with crackers or pretzel thins.

**Per serving:** 181 calories, 1.4g fat, 34.1g carbohydrates, 8.4g fiber, 6.5g sugars, 9.7g protein

## EASY BREEZY (STORE-BOUGHT) APPETIZER IDEAS

**Haute Couture Hummus:** Offer a medley of different hummus flavors with artisan or fancy pants crackers and/or beautifully cut vegetables. I also like to serve a dollop of hummus at the end of an endive leaf with a garnish on top!

**Polenta Shots:** Fill a small glass with marinara, then cut (store-bought) polenta into triangles and spear it with a festive toothpick, so the spear sits across the glass, with one point of the polenta triangle just dipping into the marinara (see pg. 89).

**Vegetable Sushi:** Sushi is a great palate cleanser and a foolproof appetizer. Buy a few rolls at your local supermarket or Asian restaurant. Put 'em on a plate and take all the credit!

**Mixed Olive Skewers:** Slide a medley of fancy pants olives onto a skewer. Add a cherry tomato for a burst of color. I'm particularly addicted to jalapeño-stuffed green olives!

# New Year's Day

I celebrate my husband's Southern heritage on New Year's Day with a festive, down-home-cookin' brunch and soul-food-inspired dinner.

In the southern part of the United States, and especially the Low Country, where my husband is from, it's customary to eat black-eyed peas, greens, and cornbread on New Year's Day for prosperity and good luck.

The black-eyed peas symbolize coins, while the greens and cornbread symbolize wealth (the color of money and gold).

You'll find these traditional dishes and other Southern favorites on my menu—all to ensure you have a happy, healthy, prosperous, and *lucky* new year!

```
┌──────────────── SOUTHERN BRUNCH MENU ────────────────┐
```

**MAIN DISH**

Whole-Wheat Drop
Biscuits (p. 58) with White
Bean Gravy (p. 60) or with
Creamed Tomatoes (p. 60)

**SIDES**

Cornbread (p. 19)
Southern Caviar (p. 60)
Black-Eyed Pea Collard Greens
(p. 61) or Creamed Kale (p. 65)

Tofu Scramble (p. 102)
Deviled "Eggs" (p. 120)

```
┌──────────── NEW YEAR'S DAY DINNER MENU ────────────┐
```

Cornbread (p. 19)
Black-Eyed Pea Collard Greens
(p. 61) or Creamed Kale (p. 65)

Cajun Tempeh Meatloaf (p. 62)
Cajun Potato Salad (p. 62) or
Deviled Potato Salad (p. 120)

Chipotle Ketchup (p. 78)

# Whole-Wheat Drop Biscuits

MAKES 5 | **Q** | **SF** | **MA** | **P** |

*Here are my quick-and-easy whole-wheat drop biscuits. For brunch, try smothering these with White Bean Gravy (p. 60) or Creamed Tomatoes (p. 60) and serving with a side of Tofu Scramble (p. 102) and a light salad or greens. Come to my house and we'll break bread—er, biscuits—together!*

1 c white whole-wheat flour
1 tsp baking powder
  pinch of salt
¼ c unsweetened applesauce
¼ c nondairy milk

1. Preheat oven to 425°F. Line a cookie sheet with parchment paper and set aside.
2. In a large mixing bowl, whisk flour, baking powder, and salt together. Stir in applesauce so large clumps of dough start to form. A light flour dusting is okay, but make sure there are no hidden flour pockets at the bottom.
3. Pour in nondairy milk, gently stirring until a wet, thick, doughy batter forms, but be careful not to overstir. Add an extra splash of liquid if necessary.
4. Drop five spoonfuls of the batter on your cookie sheet, leaving space between them. For round biscuits, use clean, wet fingers to gently and lightly smooth out each drop into a circular shape.
5. Bake for 7–10 minutes or until the biscuits are firm to the touch and golden around the edges.

▶▶▶ **CHEF'S NOTE:**
*For a savory dinner roll, add in fresh rosemary.*

**Per biscuit (plain):** 93 calories, 0.4g fat, 19.4g carbohydrates, 2.6g fiber, 2.5g sugars, 3.6g protein

## VARIATION

*Cinnamon Raisin Biscuits: For a breakfast treat, add ground cinnamon (or pumpkin pie spice) with raisins. Once baked, drizzle with my basic glaze: powdered sugar combined with a little vanilla or almond extract, and nondairy milk as needed.*

# White Bean Gravy

MAKES ABOUT 2 CUPS

| **Q** | **GF** | **SF** | **MA** | **P** |

*I really love this gravy—so much that I often eat it as a soup! (Oops!)*

- 1 15-oz can navy beans, drained and rinsed (see note)
- ¼ c vegetable broth
- 2 tbsp nutritional yeast (see note)
- ½ tsp onion powder
- ½ tsp garlic powder
- ¼ tsp Cajun Seasoning (p. 173) (see note)
- ⅛ tsp black pepper

1. Combine everything in a blender and puree until silky smooth, adding more broth as necessary to achieve the desired consistency. You don't want to thin it out too much; it should be creamy and gravy-thick.
2. Transfer to a small pot on the stove and gently heat over low until thoroughly warm.
3. Taste, adding more pepper or salt as desired.

▶▶▶ **CHEF'S NOTES:**
- *For a little kick, add another ¼ tsp Cajun Seasoning, and for a bit of a cheesy flavor, add more nutritional yeast.*
- *Any white bean, including butter beans and cannellini beans, may be substituted for the navy beans in the gravy.*

Per serving (1 cup): 169 calories, 0.4g fat, 29.4g carbohydrates, 6g fiber, 3.8g sugars, 11.1g protein

# Creamed Tomatoes

SERVES 4  | **Q** | **GF\*** | **SF** |

*This recipe comes from Katie Anderson, a lovely Herbie in West Virginia. Katie enticed me to visit her with this recipe, promising to show me how to make it. You'll find her creamed tomatoes are great at breakfast but also very versatile! They could easily be served with toast, rice, quinoa, greens, couscous, potatoes . . . anything, really! Katie says, "This recipe is not an exact science. I just do it as I go."*

- 1 28-oz can diced tomatoes, undrained
- 1½ tsp raw sugar
- ½ c nondairy milk
- 1 tbsp cornstarch
  Whole-Wheat Drop Biscuits (p. 58)*

1. Place tomatoes in a saucepan with their juices and the sugar (add more sugar if you like it sweeter or your tomatoes are very acidic).
2. Heat on medium-low for about 15–20 minutes, until hot and bubbly and the mixture has cooked down a bit.
3. In a small bowl or cup, mix nondairy milk and cornstarch together, then add to tomato mixture, and continue to cook until the mixture is thick.
4. Add salt and pepper to taste (I like it peppery) and serve poured over the biscuits.

Per serving (without biscuits): 53 calories, 0.7g fat, 11.3g carbohydrates, 2.6g fiber, 6.7g sugars, 1.9g protein

# Southern Caviar

SERVES 12  | **Q** | **GF** | **SF** | **MA** | **P** |

*This recipe comes from my mother-in-law, Cynthia Nixon. She calls it "Lower Alabama Caviar" but I've heard people call it "Texas Caviar," too, among other names. The inclusion of black-eyed peas makes this dish a perfect fuss-free appetizer or potluck dish for New Year's!*

30 oz black-eyed peas, drained and rinsed (see note)
30 oz black beans, drained and rinsed (see note)
30 oz Ro-Tel tomatoes, drained and chopped (see note)
1 green bell pepper, seeded and diced
1 yellow bell pepper, seeded and diced
1 bunch fresh parsley, minced
¼ c balsamic vinegar
2 tbsp raw sugar

1. Mix all ingredients together and allow to marinate for at least 12 hours.
2. Chill before serving.

▶▶▶ **CHEF'S NOTE**:

*Thirty-ounce jars are difficult to come by, so you may need to buy two smaller-size jars.*

**Per serving:** 156 calories, 1.3g fat, 27.1g carbohydrates, 8.2g fiber, 4.8g sugars, 9.1g protein

# Black-Eyed Pea Collard Greens

SERVES 1–2 | **Q** | **GF** | **SF** |

*This is what I serve to honor my husband's Southern heritage, along with Cornbread (p. 19) or rice. If you're dining solo, this is a great small, one-pot meal!*

1 bunch collard greens
 vegetable broth, as needed
1 small onion, sliced (white, yellow, or red)
4–6 garlic cloves, minced
½ red bell pepper, seeded and diced
1 celery stalk, diced small
 Cajun Seasoning, to taste (p. 173)
 hot sauce, to taste (e.g., Tabasco)
1 c cooked black-eyed peas

1. Drag a knife along the spine of collards to remove the stems. Then chop or tear into bite-sized pieces and set aside.
2. Line a large skillet with a thin layer of broth. Sauté the onion and garlic until the onion is soft and translucent.

3. Add bell pepper and celery, plus more broth if necessary, and cook for a minute. Add a few dashes of Cajun seasoning and hot sauce.
4. Stir and continue to cook until bell peppers have softened, adding more broth as necessary, about 3–5 minutes.
5. Add greens and use a spatula or tongs to move greens around and incorporate well. Once they're bright green (about 2–3 minutes), turn off heat.
6. Keep stirring to combine everything together. Stir in black-eyed peas, cover, and let rest for a few minutes. Add more Cajun Seasoning or hot sauce to taste. Serve over cooked grains or with a side of cornbread.

**Per serving:** 154 calories, 1.7g fat, 29.7g carbohydrates, 8.6g fiber, 3.2g sugars, 9.1g protein

# Cajun Tempeh Meatloaf

SERVES 4 | **GF** | **MA** | **PA** | **P** |

*My beloved Tempeh Meatloaf gets a Cajun makeover.*

    1   tbsp Cajun Seasoning (p. 173)
    1   red bell pepper, seeded and minced
    1   small onion, minced
    2   celery stalks, minced
    3   garlic cloves, minced
    8   oz tempeh, shredded using a cheese grater
  3-4   tbsp ketchup
    2   tbsp prepared yellow mustard
    2   tbsp nutritional yeast
    ½   tsp browning sauce (optional)
        Tabasco sauce, to taste (optional)
    1   c instant oats

1. Preheat oven to 350°F. Set aside a standard nonstick 8-inch loaf pan.
2. Mix all loaf ingredients together and let rest for 5 minutes.
3. Pack down into the loaf pan. **STOP**
4. Bake for 25–30 minutes or until firm and golden.
5. Let cool for 10–20 minutes, then serve.

**Per serving (¼ loaf):** 165 calories, 6.9g fat, 15.3g carbohydrates, 2.7g fiber, 4.8g sugars, 14.0g protein

▶▶▶ **CHEF'S NOTE:**
*I like McCormick Gourmet Collection Cajun Seasoning and Badia Louisiana Cajun Seasoning.*

# Cajun Potato Salad

SERVES 6 | **Q** | **GF**∗ | **SF**∗ | **MA** | **PA** | **P** |

*This New Orleans–inspired potato salad uses a creamy Cajun mustard as its base. It's creamy, tangy, and a little spicy.*

HOLIDAY HIT

    1   lb red potatoes, diced
        Creamy Cajun Mustard (p. 173)*
    2   tbsp chives (see note)
        vegan bacon bits (optional)
        paprika or Cajun Seasoning (p. 173) for garnish

1. Bring a large pot of water to a boil.
2. Add potatoes and cook until fork-tender, about 5 minutes.
3. Immediately rinse with cold water and let cool completely. **STOP**
4. Transfer to a mixing bowl and stir in Creamy Cajun Mustard until all the potatoes are well coated, adding more Cajun mustard as desired.
5. Toss a few times with chives or green onions to ensure even distribution and sprinkle generously with bacon bits, if using.
6. Garnish with a heavy dash of paprika or Cajun Seasoning, then cover and chill until just before serving, at least 1 hour.

▶▶▶ **CHEF'S NOTES:**
• *The dark-green parts of green onions may be substituted for the chives.*
• *To make bacon bits, combine 2 tbsp soy sauce, 1½ tsp liquid smoke, 1 tbsp water, 2 tsp pure maple syrup, ¼ tsp garlic powder, and ⅛ tsp paprika in a small saucepan and bring to a boil. Once it's boiling, immediately turn off the heat and stir in ½ cup TVP (textured vegetable protein) or TSP (textured soy protein). Continue to stir until all the liquid has been absorbed, then add salt as needed. Next you'll need to crisp up and dehydrate the bits. You can either set your toaster oven to 200°F and toast the crumbs, shaking the tray every 2*

*Cajun Potato Salad continued . . .*

*minutes to prevent burning and repeating until crisp, or fry in a nonstick pan until crispy, stirring often.*

**Per serving:** 61 calories, 0.4g fat, 12.9g carbohydrates, 1.6g fiber, 1.2g sugars, 2.1g protein

# Creamed Kale

SERVES 2-4 | **Q** | **GF** | **SF∗** |

*Traditional creamed spinach gets a healthy makeover!*

|   |   |
|---|---|
| 1 | small onion, diced |
| 5–6 | garlic cloves, minced |
| 1 | c nondairy milk (see note) |
| ¼ | c nutritional yeast |
| 2 | tsp yellow or white miso* |
| 1 | tbsp cornstarch |
| 1 | tbsp chickpea flour (optional) |
| 16 | oz frozen kale (see note) |
|   | cayenne pepper (optional) |
|   | AJ's Vegan Parmesan (p. 172) or nutritional yeast for garnish (optional) |

1. Line a large skillet with a thin layer of water (or vegetable broth) and sauté the onion and garlic over high heat until the onion is translucent and liquid has evaporated.
2. Transfer to a blender and add nondairy milk, nutritional yeast, miso, cornstarch, and chickpea flour if using. Blend until smooth and creamy, then set aside briefly.
3. Add frozen kale to the skillet and cook over high heat for 1–2 minutes until it's mostly cooked (add a tiny bit of water if necessary to prevent sticking). Once kale is nearly cooked, add milk mixture and stir to combine.
4. Continue to cook, stirring as needed, until it thickens slightly and kale is cooked completely, about 1–2 minutes.
5. Add salt and pepper to taste, plus cayenne if you like your creamed kale with a kick. Garnish with vegan Parm or nutritional yeast if desired.

▶▶▶ **CHEF'S NOTES:**

- *Unsweetened almond milk or soy milk works best in this recipe.*
- *Some brands of frozen kale are stem heavy, which I don't care for in this dish. If that's all you can find, use frozen spinach or fresh (de-stemmed and chopped) kale instead.*

**Per serving:** 84 calories, 1.8g fat, 12.7g carbohydrates, 4g fiber, 1.2g sugars, 6.3g protein

**VARIATION**

*Creamed Spinach: If you prefer the taste of spinach to kale, use that in place of the kale.*

# Tailgating & Appetizing Parties

Tailgating, Super Bowl Sunday, poker night, movie night, potlucks, kara-oke, birthday bonanzas, or just a casual '80s-themed party with friends—here are sure-to-please appetizers and finger foods for all occasions!

**A quick tip:** When building your perfect party menu, don't lose sight of the meal. A variety of different finger foods and samples is great, but sticking to a theme, and thinking about how they all come together as a meal on your guest's plate, makes you look like Martha Stewart.

## MENU

### DIPS, SPREADS & TOPPERS

"Cheese" Ball (p. 46)

Spinach & Artichoke Dip (p. 46)

No-Eggplant Caponata (p. 48)

Cowboy Caviar (p. 54)

Southern Caviar (p. 60)

Individual 7-Layer Dips (p. 68)

Mexican Dip (p. 70)

Sweet Pea Guacamole (p. 73)

### CHILIS

Rustic Chili (p. 70)

Chili Sans Carne (p. 72)

### GAME-DAY FAVORITES

Loaded Potato Skins (p. 72)

Cauliflower Hot Wings (p. 74)

Nachos Grande (p. 76)

Adobo Tostados (p. 76)

Baked Onion Rings (p. 77)

Oven Fries (p. 77) & dips

Mini Corndog Bites (p. 151)

### DESSERTS

Chocolate Chip Cookies (p. 80)

Root Beer Float Cupcakes (p. 80)

Magical Cookies (p. 83)

*You also can make plant-based burgers, sandwiches, and hot dogs, and cut them into "finger food" sizes for easy grabbing. Some great recipes to try from my Picnics, Barbecues & Outdoor Parties section (p. 130) are Quick Burgers (p. 136), Smoky Sweet Potato Burgers (p. 139), Kidney Bean–Quinoa Burgers (p. 139), Tea Party Sandwiches (see "Pinwheels & Sandwiches," p. 141), BBQ Sliders (p. 143), and Carrot Hot Dogs (p. 148).*

# Individual 7-Layer Dips

SERVES 4-6 | **Q** | **GF** | **SF**\* | **MA** | **P** |

*A seven-layer dip is an old party standby, but individual cups really dazzle!*

1    15-oz can refried beans

8    oz guacamole
     Vegan Sour Cream (p. 171) or vegan yogurt (optional)\*
     taco seasoning packet

1    12-oz jar salsa
     corn tortilla chips, baked (see note)

POSSIBLE TOPPINGS:

    green onion, sliced

    black olives, sliced

    jalapeño, seeded & sliced or finely diced small

    bell pepper (red or green), seeded & diced small

    tomato, diced

    cilantro

    pico de gallo

    vegan cheese (optional)

1. Layer in order: beans, guacamole, sour cream or yogurt (mix some taco seasoning in if desired), salsa, and toppings, then sprinkle with taco seasoning.

2. Serve with baked corn tortilla chips.

▶▶▶ **CHEF'S NOTES:**

• *Guacamole turns brown if it sits out too long, so you may want to wait until the party to add the guacamole (add it on top, then garnish with possible toppings).*

• *To bake chips yourself, cut corn tortillas into triangles and crisp in the oven for 8–10 minutes at 350°F until crisp.*

**Per serving (without toppings):** 177 calories, 75g fat, 22g carbohydrates, 73g fiber, 5.5g sugars, 8.1g protein

# Mexican Dip

MAKES 2 CUPS

| Q | GF | SF | MA | P |

*This recipe from my first cookbook,* The Happy Herbivore Cookbook, *is one of my favorite dishes to take to a party or last-minute get-together (5 minutes and we're both ready and out the door), but I find it's often overlooked—a real hidden gem!*

| | |
|---|---|
| 1 | 15-oz can cannellini beans, drained and rinsed |
| 1 | red bell pepper, seeded and stem removed |
| 1 | tbsp chili powder |
| 1 | tbsp onion flakes |
| 1½ | tsp ground cumin |
| ¼ | tsp fine salt |
| ¼ | tsp black pepper |
| | dash of garlic powder |
| | dash of paprika |
| | juice of ½ lime |
| ⅓ | c nutritional yeast |
| ⅔ | c (or less) salsa |
| 1 | jalapeño, seeded (optional) |
| ½ | c cooked black beans |

1. Preheat oven to 350°F (or you can heat this in a pot on the stove).
2. Set an 8-inch round or 9-inch square casserole dish aside.
3. Add all ingredients except black beans to a food processor.
4. Blend until smooth and transfer mixture to prepared casserole dish.
5. Gently stir in black beans and bake for 30–40 minutes or until dip is thoroughly warm. If cooking on the stove, heat over medium-low until warm, stirring often, then add beans before serving.

**Per serving (¼ c):** 80 calories, 0.9g fat, 13.8g carbohydrates, 4.4g fiber, 2.1g sugars, 5.1g protein

# Rustic Chili

SERVES 2 | Q | GF* | SF* | MA | P |

*This recipe visits from* Everyday Happy Herbivore *and offers a fresh take on chili (it's got cauliflower and no beans!)*

| | |
|---|---|
| 16 | oz brown mushrooms |
| 2 | c No-Beef Broth (p. 168)* |
| 1 | sweet onion, diced |
| 3 | garlic cloves, minced |
| 1 | 15-oz can fire-roasted diced tomatoes, undrained |
| 1 | tbsp apple cider vinegar |
| 2 | tbsp chili powder |
| 1 | tsp ground cumin |
| 1 | tsp dried oregano |
| 1 | tbsp steak sauce or ketchup |
| 2 | tsp prepared yellow mustard |
| ½ | tsp mild curry powder |
| 1 | head cauliflower, chopped into quarter-size florets |
| | cayenne pepper or hot sauce, to taste |

1. Pulse mushrooms in a blender or food processor until crumbled and the consistency of chopped olives.
2. Pour broth into a large pot, then add mushrooms, onion, and garlic, and cook over high heat for a few minutes.
3. Add tomatoes with their juices, and remaining ingredients through curry powder, stirring to combine.
4. Add cauliflower and bring to a boil.
5. Once boiling, reduce heat to low, cover, and let simmer for 10 minutes or until cauliflower is fork-tender and golden brown in color. Be sure to stir chili occasionally to incorporate everything.
6. Taste, adding cayenne pepper or hot sauce (such as Tabasco or Cholula) to taste, and season with salt and pepper.

**Per serving:** 253 calories, 2.9g fat, 46.5g carbohydrates, 15.1g fiber, 18.9g sugars, 18.1g protein

Rustic Chili

# Chili
# Sans Carne

HOLIDAY
HIT

SERVES 8 | **GF\*** | **MA** | **P** |

*Many Herbies have successfully entered this chili in cook-offs and won! (The judges have no clue it's vegan!)*

    1   small onion, diced
    1   28-oz can diced tomatoes, undrained
    2   tbsp chili powder, or to taste
    1   tsp ground cumin
    1   tsp dried oregano
    1   tsp garlic powder
    1   15-oz can kidney beans, drained and rinsed
    1   15-oz can pinto beans, drained and rinsed
    1   c frozen corn (see note)
    1   tbsp ketchup
    1   tbsp prepared yellow mustard
    1   tsp pure maple syrup
    1   tsp mild curry powder
    1   tbsp Vegan Worcestershire Sauce (p. 171)*
    2   c No-Beef Broth (p. 168)*
    1½  c TVP or TSP
        cayenne pepper, to taste (optional)
        hot sauce, to taste (optional)

1.  Line a medium pot with a thin layer of water.
2.  Add onion and cook over medium heat until translucent and most of water has evaporated, about 3 minutes.
3.  Add tomatoes with their juices, chili powder, cumin, oregano, and garlic powder and bring to a boil.

4.  Once it's boiling, reduce heat to low, cover, and let simmer for 30–45 minutes, until the liquid has reduced slightly.
5.  Add beans, corn, ketchup, mustard, maple syrup, curry powder, and vegan Worcestershire sauce, stirring to combine.
6.  Cover and turn off heat, but leave on the warm stove. Meanwhile, prepare broth.
7.  Combine broth with TVP or TSP (it'll soak up the broth and reconstitute), then add to chili, stirring to combine.
8.  Set aside chili, uncovered, for 10 minutes.
9.  Give it a good stir, then add salt and pepper to taste.
10. Add cayenne pepper or hot sauce if desired, then serve.

▶▶▶ **CHEF'S NOTE**:

*For a healthier version, try substituting brown mushrooms (coarsely chopped to the consistency of sliced olives, about 3 cups) for the TVP and reducing the broth. (See Rustic Chili recipe for help, p. 70.)*

**Per serving:** 229 calories, 1.6g fat, 37.4g carbohydrates, 11.7g fiber, 6.4g sugars, 18.2g protein

# Loaded Potato Skins

SERVES 1 | **Q** | **GF** | **SF\*** | **MA** |

*These spuds were made with Super Bowl Sunday in mind. (They also scratch the itch when you want chili-and-cheese fries!)*

    1   potato
    1   c vegetarian chili or black bean soup (see note)
    2   green onions, sliced
    1   tomato, diced
    2   tbsp corn (thawed, if using frozen)
        Vegan Sour Cream (p. 171) (optional)*
        guacamole or Sweet Pea Guacamole (p. 73) (optional)
        vegan bacon (optional)
        hot sauce

1. Steam, bake, boil, or microwave potato.
2. Place in a wide bowl or on a plate, then slice in half longways, mashing the middle.
3. Top with chili or soup, onions, tomato, corn, sour cream, guacamole, and vegan bacon if using. Drizzle generously with hot sauce.

▶▶▶ **CHEF'S NOTE:**

*You can use homemade or canned vegetarian chili or black bean soup. I typically use leftovers to make these potatoes for lunch the day after having soup or chili for dinner. For black bean soup, check out my Cuban Black Bean Soup recipe in* Happy Herbivore Abroad.

**Per serving (without optional ingredients):** 338 calories, 2.6g fat, 73g carbohydrates, 11.8g fiber, 6.3g sugars, 14.2g protein

# Sweet Pea Guacamole

MAKES 1 CUP | **Q** | **GF**✳ | **SF**✳ | **MA** | **P** |

*Peas help cut the fat of traditional guacamole while adding in an extra boost of protein and a hint of sweetness. I always serve this at summer parties and it's usually the first thing to go!*

½–1 avocado
1 c peas (thawed, if frozen)
1 tbsp onion flakes
1 tsp garlic powder
1 tsp Vegan Worcestershire Sauce (p. 171)*
 hot sauce, to taste
 juice of 1–2 lime wedges
 cilantro (optional)
½ tsp ground cumin
1 tbsp nondairy milk

1. Combine all ingredients (starting with ½ avocado) in a food processor or blender and puree until smooth, stopping to scrape sides as necessary.
2. Taste, adding more onion, garlic, Worcestershire sauce, hot sauce, lime, etc., as desired.
3. For a richer, more guacamole-like flavor, puree in the remaining avocado.

▶▶▶ **CHEF'S NOTE:**

*To keep your guacamole from turning brown, keep the avocado pit in your dip.*

**Per serving (1 tbsp, with ¼ avocado):** 27 calories, 1.3g fat, 3.1g carbohydrates, 1.3g fiber, 1.1g sugars, 0.9g protein

# Cauliflower Hot Wings

HOLIDAY HIT

SERVES 4 | **Q** | **GF** | **SF** | **PA** |

*I saw "cauliflower hot wings" on a menu in LA and, intrigued, ordered a plate for the table. It was basically deep-fried cauliflower with oil and hot sauce, but the idea behind it stayed with me. I knew I could make a better, battered wing at home. It's almost criminal that these wings are healthy. Every time I make 'em, my friends start elbowing each other out of the way. Even my husband's very omni guy friends start shoving their way to the table!*

|   |   |
|---|---|
| 1 | head cauliflower |
| ½ | c plain nondairy milk |
| ½ | c plus 1 tbsp chickpea flour |
| 1 | tbsp nutritional yeast |
|   | few dashes of onion powder |
|   | few dashes of garlic powder |
|   | cayenne pepper, to taste |
|   | dash or two of fine salt |
| 1 | tbsp plain vegan yogurt (see note) |
| ⅓ | c Frank's RedHot Original Cayenne Pepper Sauce (*not* the wing sauce) |
|   | agave nectar or honey, to taste (optional) |

1. Preheat to 450°F.
2. Line cookie sheet with parchment paper.
3. Cut cauliflower into florets (think bite-size wing pieces) and set aside.
4. Whisk nondairy milk, flour, nutritional yeast, plus a few dashes of onion and garlic powder, cayenne pepper as desired, and a dash or two salt. Stir to mix (think thick pancake batter). **STOP**
5. Dip florets into batter, let excess drip off, and place on cookie sheet. (If your cauliflower

head is huge you may need to double the batter and wing sauce.)
6. Bake for 15 minutes, until golden and fork-tender.
7. Meanwhile, whisk yogurt with Frank's and a few dashes of garlic powder. Add agave nectar or honey to taste if you want a sweet wing.
8. Once florets are finished baking, toss with hot sauce in a huge bowl and serve!

▶▶▶ **CHEF'S NOTES:**

• *I use low-fat, almond-based vegan yogurt in this recipe. Soy would also be a good option but I wouldn't use coconut or rice-based vegan yogurts.*

• *Don't have time to bake? An easier option for vegetable-based hot wings and dip is to mix hot sauce into plain vegan yogurt (I do slightly less than a 1:1 ratio) and serve with raw cauliflower and broccoli florets or tempeh strips for "wings."*

**Per serving:** 157 calories, 2.4g fat, 26.9g carbohydrates, 9.5g fiber, 7.1g sugars, 10g protein

# Nachos Grande

SERVES 1 | **Q** | **GF\*** | **SF\*** |

*Who doesn't love nachos? This is my failsafe recipe for any sports-themed party!*

### NACHOS
corn tortillas (or baked chips) (see note)
chopped or shredded lettuce
black beans or refried beans (see note)
corn, warm or chilled
tomato, diced
green onions, sliced
sliced black olives
hot sauce (optional)
guacamole (optional) (see note)
Vegan Sour Cream (p. 171) (optional)\*

### QUICK QUESO SAUCE
1   c nondairy milk
⅓   c nutritional yeast
2   tbsp whole-wheat flour\*
1   tsp onion powder
1   tsp garlic powder
½   tsp ground cumin
¼   tsp paprika
¼   tsp chili powder or cayenne (optional)
¼–⅓   c salsa

1. Cut corn tortillas into triangles and crisp in the oven for 8–10 minutes at 350°F until crisp.
2. To make the sauce, whisk all ingredients together in a saucepan, then bring to a boil over medium heat, stirring often until thick before adding the salsa.
3. Top chips with the sauce and remaining ingredients.

▶▶▶ **CHEF'S NOTES:**
• *Toss beans with hot sauce and tomatoes with lime juice for added flavor intensity. Pinto beans and fire-roasted corn add a nice twist, too!*
• *You can also make the queso ahead of time if you like.*

**Nutritional information for this recipe varies widely.**

# Adobo Tostados

SERVES 8 | **Q** | **GF** | **SF** | **PA** |

*These tostados are a Cinco De Mayo favorite on the 7-Day Meal Plans (getmealplans.com) and a stunning alternative to nachos.*

12   corn tortillas
6   oz plain vegan yogurt
2   tbsp chopped chipotle peppers in adobo sauce (optional) (see note)
½   tsp ground cumin
1   lime
⅓   c fresh cilantro
1   sweet potato, cooked and diced
1   15-oz can black beans, drained and rinsed
⅓   c corn (thawed, if frozen)
1   tomato, diced
1   avocado, sliced, or guacamole, to taste
4   green onions, sliced
    Mexican hot sauce (e.g., Cholula)

1. Toast tortillas at 350F in a toaster oven for a few minutes (until crisp) if desired.
2. Meanwhile, combine yogurt with chipotle peppers and sauce, cumin, ½ tsp lime zest, and 1 tbsp lime juice. Taste, adding more zest or juice if desired. You can also add a little cilantro, if desired. Chill until you're ready to use. (This is your adobo crema.) **STOP**
3. Spread 1–2 tbsp of the adobo crema on each tostada. Top with sweet potato, beans, plus a little sprinkling of corn, tomato, avocado, cilantro, and green onion. Drizzle with hot sauce if desired. (I like Cholula brand Chipotle Hot Sauce.) Serve.

▶▶▶ **CHEF'S NOTE:**
*You can find canned chipotle peppers in adobo sauce in the Mexican section of supermarkets.*

**Per serving:** 409 calories, 11.1g fat, 66.4g carbohydrates, 0.9g fiber, 75g sugars, 15.1g protein

# Baked Onion Rings

MAKES 30-40 | **Q** | **SF** |

*I daresay I like these better than the greasy, deep-fried kind.*

- 1 large Vidalia onion
- ½ c bread crumbs (see note)
- ½ c yellow cornmeal
- 1 tsp fine salt
- 1 tsp onion powder
- 1 tsp garlic powder
- ½ c chickpea flour
- ½ c nondairy milk

1. Preheat oven to 400°F.
2. Line a large baking sheet with parchment paper and set aside.
3. Cut onion into ⅓-inch-thick rings, reserving all large and medium rings—about 30–40 rings—and store the smaller pieces for another use.
4. Grind bread crumbs and cornmeal in mortar and pestle into a finer sand-like consistency.
5. Whisk bread crumb/cornmeal mixture, salt, and spices together in a bowl and set aside.
6. Pour chickpea flour in another bowl and nondairy milk in a third bowl.
7. Place the bowls together in a triangle, with the nondairy milk bowl pointing at you in the center.
8. Fully dip a ring in the milk, twirl it in chickpea flour until coated, then quickly dip back into the milk and immediately dredge in crumb mixture until evenly coated.
9. Place on cookie sheet and repeat with all rings.
10. Bake for 10–15 minutes until crisp and golden with a few light-brown spots on the edges, careful not to overcook or burn.
11. Sprinkle with salt and serve fresh out of the oven while the onion is still soft.

▶▶▶ **CHEF'S NOTE:**
*Make bread crumbs by tearing 1–2 slices of whole-wheat bread into equal pieces and placing in a food processor. Allow the motor to run until the bread is shredded and crumbs result. Place in a single layer on a pan and allow to air out and become stale, or toast briefly.*

**Per serving (5–7 rings):** 88 calories, 1.1g fat, 16.3g carbohydrates, 1.9g fiber, 2.3g sugars, 3.4g protein

# Oven Fries

SERVINGS VARY | **Q** | **GF** | **SF** | **PA** |

*These fries are crazy addictive fresh out of the oven. Serve them at parties with a medley of different mustards and ketchups—or \*accoutrements\* if you want to be fancy pants! (See p. 78)*

Potatoes\* (see note)

1. Preheat oven to 400°F. Line cookie sheet(s) with parchment paper and set aside.
2. Slice potatoes into shoestrings, about ½-inch thick. (Make sure they stay uniform.) **STOP**
3. Place fries on cookie sheet(s), careful not to overlap, and bake until puffed up, with a golden-brown crispy outer coating, about 8–10 minutes.
4. For extra crispness, broil at the end of baking for 30 seconds, but keep a watchful eye.

▶▶▶ **CHEF'S NOTE:**
*Other options for dipping or topping are Vegan Mayo (p. 170), which is how fries are served in the Netherlands, and British fish-and-chips style with vinegar.*

**Per serving (1 potato):** 131 calories, 0.1g fat, 29.7g carbohydrates, 3.7g fiber, 1.3g sugars, 3.4g protein

# CONDIMENTS, DIPS, DRESSINGS & MORE

Here are a few of my favorite do-it-yourself condiments that pair well with appetizers and foods ideal for dipping. The little extra work that's required is totally worth it, both in flavor and hostess points. (Your guests will be crazy impressed—just don't tell them how easy it is to make your own dippy dos.)

## Homemade Ketchup

*I'll be straight with you: homemade ketchup doesn't taste exactly like Heinz ketchup, but it's delicious in its own right and so much healthier.*

Combine 1½ tbsp tomato paste, 1–2 tbsp apple cider vinegar (or less), 2 tbsp unsweetened applesauce, 1 tsp onion powder, 1 tsp garlic powder, 2 tbsp tomato sauce, a light dash of allspice, a pinch of brown sugar (1 tsp or less), and salt to taste. Add more tomato sauce or applesauce as necessary to achieve the right consistency and texture.

## Curry Ketchup

*I tried my first vegan currywurst in Hamburg, Germany, while researching* Happy Herbivore Abroad. *While the currywurst was good, it was the accompanying sauce that really caught my attention. Curry ketchup is so simple, yet so awesome!*

Whisk ¼ cup ketchup, ½ tsp curry powder, and a dash of onion powder, paprika, and cayenne pepper together in a microwave-safe bowl. Heat in microwave for 15–30 seconds until ketchup is warm. (If you don't have a microwave, you can gently warm it in a pot on the stovetop, stirring consistently on low.) Heating the mixture helps the ketchup lose some of its sweet taste while also helping the curry flavor blend in better. Once it's warm, whisk again and taste, adding another ¼ tsp curry powder if desired.

## Chipotle Ketchup

*Chipotle classes up ketchup in a way I can't describe. It feels rustic ... artisan ... fancy pants!*

Combine ½ cup ketchup, 2 tbsp Vegan Mayo (p. 170), and chipotle powder to taste (a little goes a long way).

## Chipotle Aioli

*My husband's favorite wrap is black beans, arugula, and this aioli. It can also dress up even the most basic bean burger—a real gourmet touch!*

Combine 3 tbsp Vegan Mayo (p. 170), ½–1 tsp liquid smoke, ¼–½ tsp chipotle powder, and ⅛ tsp paprika.

## "Honey" Mustard

*This "honey" mustard makes for a great dipping sauce, condiment, or crowd-pleasing dressing. I keep a big batch of it in a small airtight container in my fridge, but it takes seconds to whip up when you need it.*

Combine equal parts Dijon mustard and honey or agave nectar (for strict vegans).

## Jane's 3-2-1 Dressing

This dressing is compliments of my good friend Jane Esselstyn. Combine 3 tbsp of balsamic vinegar, 2 tbsp of mustard (any works — try your fave) and 1 tbsp maple syrup. Whisk together until smooth. Also try other vinegars!

## Colin's Sauce

*I was talking to Dr. T. Colin Campbell's wife, Karen, and somehow we ended up on the topic of mustard. (We plant-based folk have some wild conversations!) Anyway, Mrs. Campbell mentioned that one of her husband's favorite sauces is mustard, soy sauce, and lemon juice. She noted you can change the ingredients in all different ways to create a new sauce or dressing, and it's true! This combo is now one of my favorite go-to condiments.*

Experiment with different amounts of mustard, soy sauce, and lemon juice to create the combination—or multiple combinations—that works best for you.

## Secret Sauce

*Here's a plant-based and healthy version of McDonald's famous Special Sauce.*

Add 2 parts ketchup and Vegan Mayo (p. 170) to 1 part relish and a few drops of white vinegar (optional). Add more mayo for a creamy sauce.

## Cocktail Sauce

*Cocktail sauce is most widely used as a chilled or room-temperature condiment for seafood, particularly seafood cocktail. Try serving this sauce with Crab Cakes (p. 53) or oyster mushrooms, or use it as an edgy alternative to ketchup.*

Combine 3 parts ketchup, 1 part prepared horseradish, onion powder to taste, and a squeeze of fresh lemon juice.

*Soft pretzels (p. 159) are delicious with mustard*

# Chocolate Chip Cookies

MAKES 16 | **Q** | **SF** | **MA** | **P** |

*These are the best low-fat chocolate chip cookies you'll ever eat! They're ridiculously addictive fresh out of the oven— you've been warned!*

⅓  c unsweetened applesauce
½  c light brown sugar
1  tsp vanilla extract
¼  c nondairy milk
1  c whole-wheat pastry flour
1  tsp baking powder
¼  tsp fine salt
1  tbsp cornstarch
  few dashes of ground cinnamon
½  c vegan chocolate chips

1. Preheat oven to 350°F.
2. Line a cookie sheet with parchment paper and set aside.
3. In a large bowl, combine applesauce, sugar, vanilla, and nondairy milk.
4. In a small bowl, whisk flour, baking powder, salt, cornstarch, and cinnamon.
5. Transfer the dry mixture into the wet mixture in three batches. Stir until almost combined.
6. Fold in chips.
7. Drop spoonfuls on cookie sheet and bake for 7–10 minutes for a soft and light cookie or a few minutes more for a firmer cookie, being careful not to burn.

**Per cookie:** 61 calories, 0.7g fat, 12.5g carbohydrates, 1g fiber, 6.2g sugars, 1g protein

**VARIATION**

**Double Chocolate Chip Cookies:** *Replace 2 tbsp flour with 2 tbsp unsweetened cocoa.*

# Root Beer Float Cupcakes

MAKES 12 | **SF** | **MA** | **P** |

*Root beer float cupcakes are best served with a root beer float!*

**CUPCAKES**
¼  c unsweetened applesauce
¼  c raw sugar
1  c root beer or diet root beer (see note)
1  tsp vanilla extract
1½  c whole-wheat pastry flour
1¼  tsp baking powder
½  tsp fine salt
  pinch of ground anise seed (optional)
  Suzanne's Ricemellow Creme or Vanilla Icing (see below)
  ground cinnamon or fresh nutmeg, ground, for sprinkling

**FOR THE VANILLA ICING**
1  c powdered sugar
1  tbsp nondairy milk
1  tsp vanilla extract
  food coloring (optional)

1. Preheat oven to 350°F.
2. Line muffin tin with parchment paper liners or use nonstick, and set aside.
3. In a medium bowl, whisk applesauce, sugar, root beer, and vanilla together.
4. In a large bowl, whisk flour, baking powder, salt, and anise, if using, until well combined.
5. Pour the wet mixture into the dry mixture in 3–4 batches, stirring until just combined and using as few strokes as possible.
6. Spoon batter into muffin cups to ¾ full and bake for 15–25 minutes or until a toothpick inserted into the center comes out clean.
7. Remove cupcakes from oven and transfer to a wire cooling rack.
8. If using vanilla icing, make by stirring ingredients together to combine. Add more sugar to thicken the icing or more nondairy milk to thin it out.

*Root Beer Float Cupcakes continued...*

9. Once cupcakes are completely cool, add Ricemellow Creme or vanilla icing and sprinkle with ground cinnamon or the fresh nutmeg.

▶▶▶ **CHEF'S NOTE:**
*Soda should still be carbonated and not flat.*

**Per cupcake (with regular root beer, without icing):** 83 calories, 0.2g fat, 18.2g carbohydrates, 1.6g fiber, 6.9g sugars, 1.5g protein
**Per cupcake (with diet root beer, without icing):** 75 calories, 0.2g fat, 16g carbohydrates, 1.6g fiber, 4.7g sugars, 1.5g protein

# Magical Cookies

MAKES 40  | **Q** | **GF** | **SF** | **MA** |

*This cookie recipe comes from my friends at the R&R Bakery in Marshall, Texas. I spoke in Marshall a few years ago and was gifted some of these cookies by my host. I couldn't believe they were (1) vegan, (2) made with wholesome ingredients (no oil and no sugar!), and (3) gluten-free! I begged the bakery owners to share their secret recipe with me and now they're graciously sharing it with you! (This recipe makes a lot of cookies. You can cut it in half.)*

|     |                                        |
| --- | -------------------------------------- |
| 1   | 18-oz jar smooth peanut butter (see note) |
| 3½  | c unsweetened applesauce               |
| 1¾  | tsp ground cinnamon                    |
| 3½  | tsp pure vanilla extract               |
| 3½–4 | c rolled oats (see note)              |
| 1½  | c dried cranberries (see note)         |
| 12  | oz vegan chocolate chips               |

1. Preheat oven to 350°F. Line 2 cookie sheets with parchment paper and set aside.
2. In a large bowl, mix peanut butter and applesauce until well blended.
3. Add cinnamon and vanilla and stir until well blended.

4. Add rolled oats and cranberries and mix thoroughly.
5. Add chocolate chips and mix together.
6. Use a 2-inch scoop to pick up batter and drop on parchment paper. Bake for 20–30 minutes. (The bakery uses a convection oven and it takes 20 minutes. Conventional ovens may take as long as 30 minutes.) Remove and let cool completely.

▶▶▶ **CHEF'S NOTES:**
• *From the bakery: "If you have a peanut allergy, almond butter can be substituted, but increase oats to 4 cups."*
• *My friend Chef AJ frequently caters with these cookies and prefers 4 cups oats with peanut butter, too (it will also yield more cookies). I have also substituted dried cherries for the cranberries. Yum.*

**Per cookie:** 160 calories, 9.2g fat, 16g carbohydrates, 2.5g fiber, 8.7g sugars, 4.8g protein

*Cake pops (p. 160) are another idea!*

# Romantic Occasions

Pasta and chocolate always comes to mind when I think of romantic meals (perhaps I've watched *Lady and the Tramp* too many times), but if your partner is anything like mine, the way to his/her heart is most definitely through the stomach.

Forget strawberries dipped in chocolate—if I want to show my husband how much I love him through food, then I've got to cook up his favorite Happy Herbivore meals: things like Cheater Pad Thai (from *The Happy Herbivore Cookbook*, Mini Corndog Bites (p. 151), Macaroni 'n' Cheese (see Chef's Note in Baked Mac Bites, p. 52), and Swedish Split Pea Soup (from *Happy Herbivore Abroad*) . . . not exactly what I'd always pictured myself eating by candle-light, but to each their own, I guess!

*However*, if you're still looking for that super sexy, super healthy Valentine's Day, date-night, or anniversary menu that's a bit more . . . traditional (think: chocolate, whipped cream, "steak" and champagne) here are some of my suggestions!

| MENU | |
|---|---|
| **APPETIZER** | Brown Gravy (p. 87) |
| salad—add strawberries! | grilled or steamed asparagus |
| **MAIN DISHES** | **DESSERTS** |
| Portobello Steaks (p. 86) | Cheesecake (p. 38) |
| Slow-Cooked Marinara (p. 89) | Hot Chocolate Muffins (p. 93) |
| Spaghetti alla Puttanesca (p. 89) | Dark Chocolate Truffles (p. 93) |
| Eggplant or Tofu Parm (p. 90) | Fudge Dip (p. 94) |
| No-Meat Meatballs (p. 91) with spaghetti | Cherry Tart Brownies (p. 94) |
| | Chocolate-Covered Fruits (p. 97 & 98) |
| **SIDES** | Chocolate Cake (p. 97) |
| Everyday Mushroom Gravy (p. 16) | Coconut Whipped Cream (p. 98) |
| roasted garlic mashed potatoes or Dijon | |
| mashed potatoes (p. 18) | |

# Portobello Steaks

HOLIDAY HIT

MAKES 2 | **Q** | **GF\*** | **SF\*** | **MA** |

*These portobellos are juicy and tender and make a great plant-based substitute for steak. (My Dad was a big meat guy before he went plant-based and kept asking for a vegan steak substitute. He can't get enough of these mushrooms!)*

| | |
|---|---|
| 1 | tsp dried thyme |
| 1 | tsp dried chives (optional) |
| ½ | tsp dried basil |
| ¼–1 | c No-Beef Broth (p. 168)\* or water |
| ½ | small onion, diced small |
| 1 | garlic clove, minced |
| 3 | tbsp balsamic vinegar |
| 1 | tbsp sherry or mirin |
| 2 | portobello mushrooms, de-stemmed |

1. Grind herbs to a finer consistency using a mortar and pestle (optional).

2. Line a large frying pan with a thin layer of No-Beef Broth or water.

3. Cook onion and garlic over high heat for about 2 minutes.

4. Once the liquid starts to boil, add vinegar, sherry or mirin, and ground spices.

5. Reduce heat to medium, add another ¼ cup of broth or water, and bring to a boil.

6. Add mushrooms and cook for 5 minutes.

7. Gently flip mushrooms over and cook for another 5 minutes, adding more water or broth as necessary. Repeat as necessary, cooking until mushrooms are soft and tender.

8. Remove from heat and plate.

9. Sprinkle a little salt over top and drizzle with leftover juices.

**Per steak:** 51 calories, 0.3g fat, 8.6g carbohydrates, 2.2g fiber, 3g sugars, 3.2g protein

### VARIATION

*Portobello Brisket: Portobellos also work well as a replacement for brisket (though the cook time is much shorter).*

# Brown Gravy

MAKES 2 CUPS | **Q** | **GF**✴ | **SF**✴ | **PA** |

*This is my basic brown gravy. I often serve it with Portobello Steaks and mashed potatoes, or when I don't have mushrooms on hand to make Everyday Mushroom Gravy (p. 16)*

¼  c nutritional yeast
¼  c white whole-wheat flour*
2  c vegetable broth
2  tbsp low-sodium soy sauce*
   a few dashes of pepper
1  tsp onion powder
½  tsp garlic powder

   salt, to taste
1  tbsp cornstarch (optional)
2  tbsp water (optional)

1. In a small nonstick skillet, whisk nutritional yeast and flour together and toast over medium heat until it smells toasty, about 4 minutes, but be careful not to burn.
2. Transfer to a medium saucepan and whisk in remaining ingredients through salt. `STOP`
3. Bring to a boil and allow sauce to thicken as desired and add salt to taste.
4. For an even thicker gravy, mix optional cornstarch with cold water and pour it into the gravy.

**Per serving (¼ c):** 28 calories, 0.1g fat, 5.4g carbohydrates, 0.8g fiber, 0g sugars, 1.4g protein

# Slow-Cooked Marinara

MAKES ABOUT 8 CUPS | **GF** | **SF** | **MA** | **P** |

*This is one of those dump-and-go recipes that leaves your home smelling divine! It's perfect for creating that sensual, Italian-inspired romantic setting when your partner comes home.*

    2   28-oz cans peeled tomatoes, undrained
        fresh basil, as desired
  6-8   garlic cloves, minced
    1   small onion, diced
        vegetable broth, as needed (optional)
        pinch of sugar (optional)
        pinch of red pepper flakes (optional)

1. Combine tomatoes (with juices), basil (I like a lot! I often use an entire 2-oz package), garlic, and onion in a slow cooker and cook all day (8 hours) on low or simmer over low heat on a stovetop. You should have more than enough liquid, but all slow cookers are different, so you may need to add some vegetable broth.
2. Add a pinch of sugar if it's too acidic, plus salt and pepper to taste. You can also add a pinch of red pepper flakes, if desired.

▶▶▶ **CHEF'S NOTES:**
- *This marinara freezes beautifully and leftovers are even more flavorful.*
- *If you like, you can also add other vegetables like carrots, celery, mushrooms, etc.*

**Per serving (1 c):** 49 calories, 0g fat, 10.1g carbohydrates, 2g fiber, 5.5g sugars, 2g protein

# Spaghetti alla Puttanesca

SERVES 2 | **Q** | **GF**✳ | **SF**✳ | **MA** | **P** |

*Spaghetti alla puttanesca is one of the lesser-known dishes in Italian cuisine but one of my personal favorites. It's easy to make and sure to impress! Although it's traditionally made with spaghetti, I love it with linguine, too. (My husband ordered this dish the night he told me he was moving to Boston, from South Carolina, to be with me while I was in law school. We were at a ritzy romantic Italian restaurant, so I associate this dish with love and romance more than others . . . but pasta is always romantic, right? Plus he loves this dish!).*

        Olive Tapenade (see below)
    4   oz spaghetti or linguine*
        fresh parsley, minced, for garnish

FOR THE OLIVE TAPENADE:
    1   garlic clove
    ½   c pitted kalamata olives
    2   tsp capers
    1   tbsp tomato paste
        pinch of dried oregano
        pinch of red pepper flakes
        low-sodium soy sauce (optional)*
        wine, water, or vegetable broth (optional)

1. Place Olive Tapenade ingredients in a blender or food processor with a light drizzle of soy sauce if using. Pulse a few times, adding wine, water, or broth as necessary to achieve the right consistency—it should be like a thick paste.
2. Cook pasta according to package instructions. Drain and, while pasta is still warm, mix with Olive Tapenade.
3. Garnish with fresh parsley and serve.

**Per serving:** 121 calories, 4g fat, 19.7g carbohydrates, 0.7g fiber, 1.5g sugars, 4g protein

# Eggplant Parm

SERVES 4 | **SF** |

*One recipe I'm always getting a request
for is an eggplant Parmesan dish, so here's
my healthy take on the classic Italian dish.
You can also use tofu instead of eggplant
for a meatier texture. (Tofu-style makes it
more like Chicken Parm.)*

- 2  small eggplants (see note)
- 1  c bread crumbs (see note)
- ¼  c AJ's Vegan Parmesan (p. 172)
- 2  tbsp Italian seasoning
- ¼  tsp fine salt
- ⅛  tsp pepper
- ½  c nondairy milk
- 1  tbsp cornstarch
- 1  28-oz jar marinara sauce

1. Slice eggplant into ¼–½-inch rounds. Rinse
   with water. Place a drying rack over a clean
   kitchen towel, then place eggplant slices on
   the rack.
2. Sprinkle with salt (coarse is best) and let
   rest for 30 minutes (this allows the solanine,
   which is what makes eggplant bitter, to leach
   out). Brush off salt with a damp cloth.
3. Meanwhile, preheat oven to 350°F. Line
   a cookie sheet with parchment paper and
   set aside.
4. Combine bread crumbs, vegan Parmesan,
   Italian seasoning, salt, and pepper, then grind
   in a food processor or with a mortar and pestle
   to a fine, sand-like consistency. Pour crumb
   mixture into a shallow bowl.
5. Whisk nondairy milk and cornstarch together,
   then pour into another shallow bowl.
6. Dip each eggplant round into the nondairy
   mixture, briefly submerging it, then immediately into the bread-crumb mixture. Flip
   eggplant over and press into the bread

crumbs again, repeating as necessary so it is
well coated.

7. Repeat with remaining eggplant slices,
   placing each finished product on the
   cookie sheet.
8. Bake for 12 minutes. Flip them over and bake
   for 5–10 minutes more. If necessary, bake for
   another 5–10 minutes, flipping them halfway through. Bake until eggplant rounds
   are soft and crumbs have taken on a deeper,
   more golden coloring—but be careful not to
   burn (time may vary based on how thick your
   slices are).
9. Arrange eggplant slices on a plate, cover
   with marinara sauce, and garnish with
   vegan Parmesan.

▶▶▶ **CHEF'S NOTES:**

- *Skin is optional on the eggplant. Some people like
  it, some people find it too chewy.*
- *Make bread crumbs by tearing 1–2 slices of whole-
  wheat bread into equal pieces and placing in a food
  processor. Allow the motor to run until the bread is
  shredded and crumbs result. Place in a single layer
  on a pan and allow to air out and become stale, or
  toast briefly.*
- *Working with ¼ cup bread-crumb mixture at a
  time prevents the breading from becoming too wet.
  If the breading becomes too moist, it won't stick.*

**Per serving (without marinara sauce):** 202 calories, 5.5g fat, 33.3g
carbohydrates, 10.4g fiber, 8.4g sugars, 7.6g protein

## VARIATION

***Tofu Parm:*** *Substitute 15 oz extra-firm tofu for
the eggplants. Drain and press the tofu by wrap-
ping the tofu in a clean kitchen cloth and placing
it between two cutting boards. Place a large, heavy
object on the top board. Allow to rest for 20 minutes,
forcing excess water out of the tofu. Turn tofu on
its side and cut 12 evenly sized cutlets. Use in place
of eggplant, above, baking for 12 minutes, then 10
minutes on the other side.*

# No-Meat Meatballs

MAKES 16 | **Q** | **GF**∗ | **SF**∗ | **MA** | **PA** | **P** |

*These are my favorite no-meat meatballs (or "bean balls" as we sometimes call them). They pair perfectly with spaghetti and pasta sauce for a romantic meal, but you can also use them in any recipe calling for meatballs. My husband especially loves putting leftover meatballs in a bun with marinara for a "meatball sub" experience.*

| | |
|---|---|
| 1 | 15-oz can kidney beans, drained and rinsed |
| ¼ | medium onion |
| 2 | garlic cloves, peeled |
| 1 | carrot, skinned |
| 1 | c cooked brown rice |
| 2 | tbsp ketchup |
| 2 | tbsp steak sauce |
| 1–2 | tbsp low-sodium soy sauce∗ |
| 1 | tbsp Dijon mustard |
| 1 | tbsp Italian seasoning |
| 1½ | tsp Vegan Worcestershire Sauce (p. 171)∗ |
| | hot sauce, to taste |
| ¾ | c instant oats (see note) |

1. Preheat the oven to 350°F. Line a cookie sheet with parchment paper and set aside.
2. Mash kidney beans with a fork in a mixing bowl until mostly pureed, but with some half beans and bean parts remaining, then set aside.
3. Pulse onion and garlic cloves in a food processor until minced (but do not puree or pulverize) and transfer to mixing bowl.
4. Repeat with carrots and transfer to mixing bowl.
5. Pulse or grind brown rice so that it is coarsely chopped, and transfer to your mixing bowl.
6. Add ketchup, steak sauce, soy sauce, Dijon mustard, Italian seasoning, Worcestershire sauce, and a few dashes of hot sauce, stirring to combine. **STOP** Stir in oats.
7. Use your hands to shape into walnut-size meatballs.
8. Bake for 20–30 minutes or until the meatballs are golden brown on the outside. Let cool for 10–15 minutes—they firm as they cool.

▶▶▶ **CHEF'S NOTE:**

*If you do not have instant oats, pulse rolled oats in food processor to chew them up a bit.*

**Per meatball:** 81 calories, 0.8g fat, 15.8g carbohydrates, 2.7g fiber, 13g sugars, 3g protein

# Hot Chocolate Muffins

SERVES 12 | **Q** | **SF** | **MA** | **P** |

*I'm totally obsessed with adding cayenne pepper (or chipotle powder) to chocolate and calling it "hot chocolate." (Well, it is hot chocolate!) I love these muffins!*

- 1¾ c white whole-wheat flour
- ¼ c unsweetened cocoa
- 1 tbsp baking powder
- ¼ tsp fine salt
- ½ c brown sugar
- ¼ tsp cayenne pepper (or chipotle) powder
- ½ c unsweetened applesauce (see note)
- ½ c nondairy milk (see note)
- ¼ c water
- 1 tsp vanilla extract

1. Preheat oven to 350°F.
2. Line a muffin tin with parchment paper cups or use nonstick.
3. In a mixing bowl, whisk flour, cocoa, baking powder, salt, sugar, and cayenne together.
4. Add applesauce, nondairy milk, water, and vanilla.
5. Taste, adding more cayenne or chipotle if desired (a little goes a long way! It also mellows slightly during baking.)
6. Spoon into muffin cups and bake 15–20 minutes, until a toothpick inserted in the center comes out clean.

▶▶▶ **CHEF'S NOTES:**

- *For a moister muffin, add another ¼ cup applesauce.*
- *For a richer muffin, use chocolate nondairy milk.*

**Per muffin:** 101 calories, 0.5g fat, 22.6g carbohydrates, 12g fiber, 7g sugars, 2.3g protein

# Dark Chocolate Truffles

MAKES 10 | **Q** | **GF** | **SF** | **MA** | **P** |

*These good-for-you truffles are only 39 calories a pop! Make them for your sweetheart.*

- 1 c cooked white beans (see note)
- 1 tbsp smooth peanut butter
- 1 tbsp pure maple syrup, plus more to taste
- 2 tbsp unsweetened cocoa

1. Combine all ingredients in a food processor and allow motor to run. Stop to scrape the sides as necessary, until you have a smooth and homogenous mixture.
2. Taste, adding another 1 tbsp maple syrup for a sweeter chocolate (you don't want it to get too wet, though). The "batter" should be thick and pliable.
3. Pick off 10 pieces and roll into bouncy bite-size balls.

▶▶▶ **CHEF'S NOTES:**

- *Any white beans, such as navy, cannellini, or butter beans, will work in this recipe.*
- *If you want to get all fancy pants, roll crushed vegan chocolate chips or nut pieces into the balls.*

**Per truffle:** 39 calories, 1g fat, 6.2g carbohydrates, 18g fiber, 14g sugars, 2g protein

You may also need to add another 1 tbsp agave nectar for your taste. The end result should be the consistency of thick icing.

▶▶▶ **CHEF'S NOTES:**
- *Any white beans, such as navy, cannellini, or butter beans may be used here.*
- *For my sweetener-free friends, you can use ⅓–½ cup soaked dates instead of agave nectar: just blend them with ¼ cup nondairy milk or water first (it will form a paste) and add with the beans and cocoa.*

**Per serving (2 tbsp):** 80 calories, 0.6g fat, 16.7g carbohydrates, 3.6g fiber, 4.5g sugars, 4.5g protein

# Fudge Dip

MAKES 2 CUPS │ **Q** │ **GF** │ **SF** │ **MA** │ **P** │

*This easy fudge dip makes for a healthy "chocolate fondue" alternative. Start dipping those fruits! (P.S. Kids love it with apple slices!)*

- 1 15-oz can white beans, drained and rinsed (see note)
- ¼ c unsweetened cocoa plus more to taste
- 2 tbsp agave nectar, plus more to taste (see note) nondairy milk

1. Blend beans with cocoa and agave nectar in a food processor or strong blender until well combined. Add a splash of nondairy milk as necessary to achieve a creamed consistency.
2. Taste, adding cocoa 1 tbsp at a time until you're satisfied with the richness. I like it at 6 tbsp, but my dark-chocolate-loving testers went up to as much as 8 tbsp (½ cup total).

# Cherry Tart Brownies

SERVES 9 │ **Q** │ **SF** │ **MA** │ **P** │

*These brownies are thin and a bit tart. The batter is addictive—you've been warned.*

- 1 c white whole-wheat flour
- 6 tbsp unsweetened cocoa
- ½ c brown sugar
- 1 tsp baking powder
- 1 c frozen (pitted) cherries, thawed (see note)
- 1 tbsp balsamic vinegar (or chocolate balsamic)
- 1 tbsp molasses (*not* blackstrap)
- 1 c water
  chocolate chips for sprinkling (optional)

1. Preheat oven to 350°F.
2. Whisk dry ingredients together.
3. Pulse cherries a few times in a food processor or coarsely chop.
4. Add to dry mix with remaining ingredients. Stir to combine and bake for 25 minutes.

▶▶▶ **CHEF'S NOTE:**
*I use frozen dark sweet cherries.*

**Per brownie:** 98 calories, 0.8g fat, 23g carbohydrates, 4.2g fiber, 10.7g sugars, 2.6g protein

# Chocolate-Covered Bananas

SERVES 1 | **Q** | **GF** | **SF** | **MA** |

*Nothing says romance like chocolate-dipped fruits.*

> 1  banana
>    chocolate
>    toppings (optional)

1. Skewer ½ a banana on a Popsicle stick.
2. Wrap in plastic wrap and freeze until solid, about 3 hours.
3. Line a cookie sheet with wax or parchment paper.
4. Melt chocolate (see note on page 98) and pour into a deep glass.
5. Set out additional toppings such as chopped nuts, coconut flakes, or sprinkles in shallow bowls, if using.
6. Dip frozen banana into chocolate, swirling so they are completely covered.
7. Roll in additional toppings such as peanuts or sprinkles immediately, if additional toppings are desired.
8. Place coated banana on parchment paper and let cool. (You can also speed this along by popping them back in the freezer or fridge.)

**1 banana with 1 oz chocolate:** 257 calories, 8.4g fat, 43.7g carbohydrates, 4.5g fiber, 28.6g sugars, 3.3g protein

# Chocolate Cake

HOLIDAY HIT

SERVES 9 | **Q** | **GF\*** | **SF** | **MA** | **P** |

*Balsamic vinegar is the secret to chocolate cake. (You'll see!) This cake is cheap, quick, and sure to please.*

> 1¼  c white whole-wheat flour
> ¼   c unsweetened cocoa
> 1   tsp baking soda
> ½   tsp baking powder
>     pinch of salt (optional)
> ½   c brown sugar
> 1   c nondairy milk (plain or chocolate)
> 6   tbsp unsweetened applesauce
> 2   tbsp balsamic vinegar
> 1   tsp chocolate or pure vanilla extract
> ¼   c vegan chocolate chips

1. Preheat oven to 375°F. Set aside an 8-inch square nonstick cake pan or round springform pan.
2. In a mixing bowl, whisk together flour, cocoa, baking soda, baking powder, and salt (if using).
3. Add sugar, nondairy milk, applesauce, balsamic vinegar, and chocolate or vanilla extract, stirring until just combined.
4. Transfer batter to your pan and sprinkle with chocolate chips.
5. Bake for 20–30 minutes, until cake springs back to the touch and a toothpick inserted in the center comes out clean.

**Per serving:** 128 calories, 2.3g fat, 25.2g carbohydrates, 2.9g fiber, 11.9g sugars, 3.2g protein

# Chocolate-Covered Strawberries

SERVES 1 | **GF** | **SF** | **MA** | **P** |

*A tad time consuming, but easy to make and sure to wow and dazzle your sweetheart. To go extra fancy pants, melt vegan white chocolate, dip your fork into it, and then drizzle the white chocolate back and forth over your prepared chocolate dipped strawberries.*

> strawberries
> chocolate

1. Line a cookie sheet with wax or parchment paper.
2. Melt chocolate (see below) and dip strawberry into chocolate, swirling to coat.
3. Place on parchment paper and let set, at least 30 minutes.

**▶▶▶ CHEF'S NOTES:**

- *How to Melt Chocolate: Place chocolate in heatproof bowl. Fill a saucepan with a couple inches water and bring to a simmer over medium heat. Turn off heat and set your metal chocolate-filled bowl in the water (it should float). Once chocolate starts to melt, stir so it's smooth and completely melted. (Alternatively, you can use a double boiler if you have one.) You could also try melting chocolate in the microwave in a microwave-safe bowl, heating in 10-second intervals and stirring between.*
- *For a fun gift, stick long skewers into the strawberries to make a bouquet.*

**Per chocolate-covered strawberry:** 54 calories, 2.8g fat, 6.5g carbohydrates, 0.6g fiber, 5.5g sugars, 0.8 protein

# Coconut Whipped Cream

SERVES 24 | **GF** | **SF** | **MA** |

*Coconut milk whipped cream has taken the Internet by storm! Since it's made from coconut milk, it's high in both fat and calories, but I figure whipped cream is one of those foods that's always an indulgence anyway. Enjoy!*

> 1   14-oz can coconut milk
> powdered sugar, to taste (optional)
> pure vanilla extract (optional), to taste

1. Place a can of coconut milk upside down in your fridge (leave it there overnight to have a slumber party with your kale).
2. When you open the can, there will be a firm, waxy layer on top. Scoop this out. (There will be water under it, which you should discard or save for another use later—you only want the solid cream part.)
3. Beat the cream with electric beaters at high speed for a few minutes until it becomes light and fluffy (you can also beat in a touch of sugar and vanilla extract, if desired).

**Nutritional information is not possible for this recipe.**

# Brunch

Sundays with friends, church potlucks, Easter morning, baby showers, bridal showers, Mother's Day, conferences, and more . . . there are so many wonderful plant-based options when breakfast or brunch is in order. Admittedly, when I hear the word "brunch" I think "big breakfast" but brunches can still be lunch-like. If your brunch is later in the afternoon or you want to have a few savory options that aren't traditional brunch foods, add a healthy green salad (add fruit like orange slices or strawberries to feel lighter and more breakfast-y), and serve Tea Party sandwiches (p. 141) or other wraps.

Whatever you choose, you'll be delighted to find nearly every brunch item can be made ahead and travels beautifully!

## MENU

**APPETIZER**

salad—add strawberries
and citrus fruits!

**MAIN DISHES**

Tofu Scramble (p. 102)

French Toast (p. 105) or Fluffy
Pancakes & Waffles (p. 105)

**SIDES**

Home Fries (p. 103)

Fruit Salad (p. 106) or fruit

**DRINK**

Bloody Mary (p. 109) or
Mimosa (p. 109)

*Want more options? There's also
a great Southern Brunch Menu in
the New Year's Day section (p. 58).*

# Tofu Scramble

SERVES 2 | **Q** | **GF** | **SF\*** | **MA** | **P** |

*Tofu Scramble is a great replacement
for scrambled eggs, and it's even easier
to make! Anytime I'm having a brunch
party, this dish is first on my list. Throw
in whatever leftover greens, vegetables, or
beans you have in your fridge to extend the
meal or dazzle guests! (Think in color!)*

    15  oz firm tofu* (see note)
     3  tbsp nutritional yeast
     1  tbsp Dijon mustard
     1  tsp onion powder
     1  tsp garlic powder
    ½  tsp ground cumin
    ¼  tsp turmeric
        vegetables, greens, etc. (optional)
        black salt (optional)

1. Drain tofu and mash in a skillet with a potato
   masher (or crumble with your hands).
2. Stir in all ingredients from nutritional yeast
   through turmeric and cook over high heat,
   adding a splash of water or nondairy milk
   to prevent sticking if necessary. Continue to
   cook until tofu is yellow and warm.
3. Add in greens and/or other vegetables and
   cook until greens have softened and other
   vegetables are warm.

4. If using, add black salt (for an eggy taste), hot
   sauce, and salsa, plus salt and pepper to taste.

▶▶▶ **CHEF'S NOTE:**

*For a soy-free scramble, instead of using tofu, use
mashed (already cooked) little red-skin potatoes with
Dijon mustard and black salt; they taste a lot like eggs
that way. Plain hummus mixed in (to taste) also helps
achieve that egginess.*

**Per serving:** 121 calories, 2.3g fat, 7.1g carbohydrates, 1.8g fiber, 1.8g
sugars, 18.9g protein

**VARIATIONS**

• *Tofu Frittata:* Preheat oven to 400°F. Set aside
  a shallow glass 9-inch pie dish. Prepare Tofu
  Scramble (do not cook, just mix, but make sure
  it's crumbled really well), and transfer to pie dish.
  Pat mixture down firmly with a spatula. Bake for
  20–25 minutes, until the top is golden brown. Let
  cool for 5–10 minutes. Place a dish over the top
  and quickly, but gently, flip frittata out. Only 67
  calories per serving!
• *Tofu Quiche:* Preheat oven to 350°F. Set aside a
  shallow glass 9-inch pie dish or square baking pan.
  Add another 1 tbsp nutritional yeast plus ¼ cup
  cornstarch. Combine all ingredients (except
  mix-ins) in a blender or food processor and puree
  until smooth, thick, and creamy. Stir in your addi-
  tions, transfer to pie dish, and bake for 30–40
  minutes, until golden in color and center is firm.
  Allow to cool for at least 10 minutes. See also Mini
  Soy-Free Quiche (p. 128). Tofu Quiche is only 84
  calories per serving.

# Home Fries

SERVINGS VARY | **Q** | **GF** | **SF** |

*Yes! Oven-roasted home fries are possible without oil! The trick to getting seasonings to stick? Damp potatoes. My favorite "home fries" are made from sliced fingerling potatoes with fresh thyme, fresh chopped rosemary, and black pepper (sometimes I also add lemon zest). Other options are diced russet potatoes with Italian seasoning or sweet potatoes with cinnamon, garam masala, Chinese five-spice powder, or taco seasonings.*

chopped potatoes (see note)
seasonings

1. Preheat oven to 400°F. Line a baking sheet with parchment paper.
2. In a colander, run chopped potatoes under water and then shake off any excess water (you don't want soaked potatoes, just slightly wet).

3. Add potatoes to your baking sheet and season generously. Toss to coat, and sprinkle again if desired (it's okay to be generous with herbs and spices, except hot spices—be careful with those).
4. Bake until fork-tender (about 25–40 minutes, depending on potato size), then broil at the end to get a nice crispness. (Keep an eye on the oven as you broil—potatoes burn fast! It shouldn't take more than a minute but all ovens and potatoes are different.)

▶▶▶ **CHEF'S NOTES:**

- *If you plan to roast in a glass casserole dish, line with a thin layer of broth, white wine, or a lighter-colored beer. Just remember to give it a good stir to incorporate before serving. (Depending on how long you bake, the beer or wine flavoring may be strong or subtle.)*
- *I like adding diced apple when making "sweet" sweet potato home fries.*
- *It's a bit tricky estimating how many potatoes to use per person, because it depends on the type of potato you use. However, if you have very large potatoes, estimate 1 per person. If your potatoes are smaller, estimate 2 potatoes per person.*

**Per serving (1 potato):** 131 calories, 0.1g fat, 29.7g carbohydrates, 3.7g fiber, 1.3g sugars, 3.4g protein

## MEXICAN RANCHEROS
### (AKA HANGOVER FOOD)

If you want to start the morning off with a kick (or maybe there was too much partying the night before?), try whipping up a quick meal of Tofu Scramble (p. 102) with some jalapeños or chili peppers diced into the mix and Home Fries. Serve with some refried beans, corn tortillas, guacamole, and salsa—and some strong coffee!

# French Toast

SERVES 4 | **Q** | **SF** |

*When my husband and I first started dating, he surprised me with homemade French toast. (I knew right then he was a keeper!) After we went plant-based, I tasked him with creating a vegan version—I like this one even better!*

| | |
|---|---|
| 8 | slices of whole-wheat bread |
| 1 | c nondairy milk |
| ¼ | c chickpea flour |
| 1 | tsp ground cinnamon |
| 1 | tsp pure maple syrup |
| ½ | tsp fine salt |
| ¼ | tsp ground nutmeg |
| ¼ | tsp pure vanilla extract (optional) |
| | powdered sugar for dusting, if desired |

1. Cut bread in half diagonally while nonstick skillet heats.
2. Whisk remaining ingredients except powdered sugar together in a shallow, wide bowl.
3. When skillet is ready (a drop of water will fizzle), dip a few bread slices into the milk. Transfer to skillet and cook for 3 minutes, pressing the bread down with the back of a nonstick-safe spatula. Flip over and cook for 3 more minutes. Scrape away any bits in skillet, then repeat with the other bread slices.
4. Sprinkle with powdered sugar, if desired.

**Per serving (4 triangles):** 198 calories, 3.3g fat, 32.6g carbohydrates, 6.6g fiber, 5.5g sugars, 9.9g protein

# Fluffy Pancakes & Waffles

HOLIDAY HIT

MAKES 8 | **Q** | **SF** |

*I love pancakes (and waffles!), especially for dinner. Here's my basic pancake recipe from* The Happy Herbivore Cookbook.

| | |
|---|---|
| 1 | c white whole-wheat flour |
| 1 | tbsp baking powder |
| ½ | tsp ground cinnamon |
| ⅛ | tsp fine salt |
| 1 | c nondairy milk |
| 2 | tbsp pure maple syrup |
| 1 | tbsp raw sugar (optional) |

1. In a mixing bowl, whisk flour, baking powder, cinnamon, and salt together.
2. Add nondairy milk, maple syrup, and sugar, if using. Stir to combine. Let rest for 10 minutes. Transfer to a large liquid measuring cup or use ¼ cup measuring cup.
3. Heat nonstick skillet over high heat. When a drop of water fizzles, it's ready.
4. Reduce heat to low and pour in ¼ cup batter. Cook until bubbles form. Gently slide nonstick safe spatula underneath, gently flip, and cook for 2–3 minutes more. Repeat.

### VARIATIONS

- *Chocolate: Replace ¼ cup flour with cocoa, omit cinnamon, and sub agave for the maple. Top with peanut butter or strawberry jam.*
- *Pumpkin: Omit cinnamon and maple syrup. Add ¼ cup canned pure pumpkin and ½ tsp pumpkin pie spice.*

### ⫸ CHEF'S NOTE:

- *Here's my basic waffle batter recipe from* Happy Herbivore Abroad*: 1 cup whole-wheat pastry flour, ¼ tsp ground cinnamon, ¼ tsp fine salt, 2 tsp baking powder, dash of ground nutmeg, 1 cup nondairy milk, and ¼ tsp pure vanilla extract.*
- *Several fans have also written me that my pancake batters in other Happy Herbivore cookbooks work as a waffle batter.*

**Per pancake:** 79 calories, 0.5g fat, 16.3g carbohydrates, 1.7g fiber, 3.7g sugars, 2.3g protein

# Fruit Salad

*The trick to making an amazing fruit salad is to (1) use seasonal fruits (preferably organic—they taste better) and (2) use lots of color and variety! The more fruits and colors the better!*

CLASSIC Diced strawberries with blueberries, banana slices, and fresh mint. Add orange juice for a hint of sweetness (or lime juice for a twist!)—just don't add bananas until the very end or they'll turn brown.

TRIFECTA My pal Chef AJ does an amazing "trifecta" salad of strawberries, bananas, grapes (both colors), and coconut flakes.

THEMED Single-color fruit salads dazzle at themed events. For example, cherries, strawberries and raspberries make for a pretty Valentine's Day or wedding spread.

FOR KIDS Make the face of beloved Sesame Street friends using fruit (or vegetables): strawberries for Elmo, blueberries for Cookie Monster, pineapple for Big Bird, broccoli for Oscar the Grouch, and so on. (Do a quick internet search.)

KABOBS Strawberry, cantaloupe, pineapple, kiwi, and 2–3 blueberries (it looks like an arrow). See opposite page.

POOLSIDE Frozen melon balls (watermelon, cantaloupe, and honeydew melons) plus frozen grapes cool off summer heat! Kids love these, too!

## BREAKFAST BRUSCHETTA

When you're craving something a little fruity, try this beautifully colorful spin on bruschetta: Slather toasted bread with vegan yogurt, such as my Tofu Yogurt (p. 170) or store-bought, and top with fresh fruit such as bananas, strawberries, kiwi, peaches, or blueberries. Fresh mint is another lovely addition, or try adding a little orange juice or zest mixed into the yogurt.

# Bloody Mary

SERVES 2 | **Q** | **GF\*** | **SF\*** | **MA** | **P** |

*What adult brunch is completely without a Bloody Mary? Since most of the commercial Bloody Mary mixes are filled with scary ingredients, I created my own version using tomato sauce. It's so easy to make! (And delicious as a virgin drink, too!)*

    Bloody Mary mix (see below)
    celery salt or black salt for the rim (optional)
    ice
1½  oz vodka (optional)
 1  lime wedge
 1  lemon wedge
    green olives with brine (optional)
 1  celery stalk

    **FOR THE BLOODY MARY MIX:**
 8  oz water
 8  oz tomato sauce
 1  tbsp hot sauce
1½  tsp Dijon mustard
1½  tsp Vegan Worcestershire Sauce (p. 171)\*
 ¼  tsp onion powder
 ¼  tsp garlic powder
 ¼  tsp black pepper
    celery seed, to taste (optional)

1. To make Bloody Mary mix, whisk water, tomato sauce, hot sauce, Dijon mustard, Worcestershire sauce, and spices together. Taste, adding more hot sauce, Dijon, or spices as desired. (I like my cocktail with a kick, so I tend to add another ½ tsp Dijon and several dashes of black pepper and/or hot sauce).
2. To make the cocktail, garnish rims of two high-ball glasses or two tall, narrow drink glasses with celery salt or black salt (optional).
3. Fill with ice, add vodka, and pour Bloody Mary mix over top.

4. Garnish with lime, lemon, green olives, and a splash of brine, if using, and then stir with the celery stalk.

▶▶▶ **CHEF'S NOTE:**

*I've also been served a pickle, a single green bean, and an asparagus spear instead of celery stalk at restaurants. Keep it fun and interesting!*

**Per serving (without green olives):** 169 calories, 0.8g fat, 15.2g carbohydrates, 4.1g fiber, 10.8g sugars, 3.7g protein

# Mimosa

SERVINGS VARY | **Q** | **GF** | **SF** | **MA** | **P** |

*The classic brunch drink! For a twist, try serving grapefruit juice instead. For a nonalcoholic version, swap in ginger ale.*

    fresh orange juice
    champagne

1. Combine equal parts fresh orange juice with champagne (or other sparkling wine) and chill.
2. Serve in champagne flute.

**Per serving (1 c):** 142 calories, 0.2g fat, 14g carbohydrates, 0g fiber, 10.4g sugars, 0.8g protein

# Breakfast in Bed

All through my childhood and even during high school my parents served me breakfast in bed. I was one lucky little lady. It was rare I ate breakfast at the table and surely miss those days of being my Mom's little "queenie."

There's just something special about eating in bed! It's cozy, sweet, loving, romantic . . . and it's what I love about room service!

The breakfast in bed menu (on the next page) comes together in just 10 minutes! (Easy to pull together while your sweetie sleeps!) Don't forget to include juice and coffee or tea—and a flower!

Oatmeal for All Occasions

MENU

Tofu Scramble (p. 102)
Muesli (Overnight Oats) (p. 113) or Oatmeal for All Occasions (p. 113)
Parfait (p. 114)
sliced fresh fruit
toast with jam or French Toast (p. 105)

# Muesli (Overnight Oats)

SERVES 1 | **Q** | **GF** | **SF** | **MA** | **P** |

*I love muesli, especially during the hot summer. It's cool, easy, and refreshing. Muesli is also my go-to option when I'm catering or when I'm expecting several guests for breakfast, since I can assemble individual portions in jars the night before.*

⅓ c rolled oats
½–⅔ c nondairy milk
fresh fruit, diced

1. Combine oats with nondairy milk (⅔ cup makes it a little soupy, which I prefer).
2. Chill overnight or for at least 2 hours. It gets thick, almost like yogurt.
3. Stir in diced fresh fruit, such as apple, pear, peach, banana, grapes, or strawberries, before serving, and enjoy.

**CHEF'S NOTE:**
*For a very creamy, almost pudding-like version, add chia seeds.*

**Per serving (½ c nondairy milk, without fruit):** 123 calories, 3.2g fat, 19.5g carbohydrates, 3.2g fiber, 0g sugars, 4.1g protein

# Oatmeal for All Occasions

SERVES 1 | **Q** | **GF*** | **SF** |

*Oatmeal's versatility allows you to get all fancy pants with flavored toppings for different holidays (see next page). Here is my basic oatmeal recipe along with some of my favorite "holiday" oatmeal toppings, all courtesy of my 7-Day Meal Plan service (getmealplans.com).*

½ c rolled oats* (see note)
¾ c water

1. Combine oats and water in a small saucepan, adding more water if you like your oatmeal to be a little soupy. (If using frozen or dried fruits, add with oats and water.)
2. Bring to a boil, reduce heat to medium, and continue to cook, stirring regularly, until you have oatmeal.
3. Add other ingredients (see add-on options), stir to combine, and then garnish, if desired.

**CHEF'S NOTE:**
*You can add a little nondairy milk at the end for a creamier oatmeal.*

**Per serving (without add-ons):** 150 calories, 3g fat, 27g carbohydrates, 4g fiber, 1g sugars, 5g protein

*Oatmeal For All Occasions continued . . .*

## VARIATIONS

**VALENTINE'S DAY DOUBLE CHOCOLATE** *2 tbsp unsweetened cocoa, ½ banana (or ½ cup frozen pitted cherries), 1 tbsp chocolate chips (total 288 calories)*

**ST. PADDY'S GREEN APPLE** *½ green apple, ¼ cup applesauce, ground cinnamon to taste, 1½ tbsp brown sugar (total 281 calories)*

**EASTER BUNNY BLUEBERRY** *¼ c applesauce, 1⅓ cups frozen blueberries, 1 tsp lemon zest (or to taste) (total 293 calories)*

**PATRIOTIC OATMEAL** *Muesli (Overnight Oats) (p. 113) with ¾ cup blueberries, ½ banana, 1 cup strawberries (total 290 calories)*

**BACK TO SCHOOL—PB&J** *¼ cup applesauce, 1 tbsp jam, 1½ tbsp peanut butter (total 284 calories)*

**HALLOWEEN PUMPKIN** *¼ cup pure pumpkin, ¼–½ tsp pumpkin pie spice, 2 tbsp raisins, 1 tbsp pure maple syrup (total 284 calories)*

**THANKSGIVING CRANBERRY-APPLE** *¼ cup cranberries, ½ sliced apple, ¼ cup unsweetened applesauce, 1 tbsp pure maple syrup (total 283 calories)*

**CHRISTMAS CHAI** *Steep 1 chai tea bag in ¾–1 cup water. Cook oatmeal in Chai tea instead of water. Add ½ sliced banana, ¼ cup blueberries or raspberries, 1 tbsp pure maple syrup, plus garam masala (or pumpkin pie spice) to taste (total 282 calories)*

**NEW YEAR'S CINNAMON RAISIN** *3 tbsp raisins, ¼ cup applesauce, 1 tsp pure maple syrup, ground cinnamon to taste (total 281 calories)*

**BIRTHDAY CAKE** *½ mashed banana, 1 tsp vanilla pudding mix or protein powder (or to taste), dollop of vegan yogurt, 1 tsp sprinkles (total 280 calories)*

# PERFECT PARFAITS

I love parfaits because they're easy and adaptable! Not only do parfaits fit any occasion (they dazzle at breakfast, accent a luncheon, and shine as a dessert after dinner), but you can also change the ingredients to fit *any* occasion. Just capture the color or spirit of the occasion with your ingredients.

For example, if it's a baby shower for a boy, use blueberries to make it festive. A romantic breakfast-in-bed or Valentine's Day party? Use strawberries and shaved chocolate. Hosting a luau? Add pineapple and coconut flakes. Capture the color or spirit of the occasion with your ingredients—kiwi is totally cool on St. Paddy's Day. Utilize different size glasses (e.g., shot glasses, champagne flutes, ice cream dishes, and wine glasses) to create even more options without having to buy anything special.

Fresh fruit, granola, or rolled oats (or crushed cookies or graham crackers), and vegan yogurt are the ticket. Simply layer, layer, layer. For those of you who love a good formula: 3 parts fruit, 1 part crunch, 3 parts creaminess.

It's pretty easy to come by commercial vegan yogurts these days, but you can also make it yourself from tofu (p. 170)!

# GET WELL SOON MENU

Being under the weather is about as opposite from "celebration" and "special occasion" as you can get, but comfort foods like this Feel-Better Soup will definitely lighten your spirits—or the spirit of a sick loved one. Other hot remedies for under-the-weather times include Chickpea Noodle Soup (p. 151) or a Hot Toddy (p. 37) comfort foods to cheer up a sick friend or self include Baked Mac Bites (p. 52) and Chocolate Shake (p. 156; P.S. This is the only thing I can stand when my stomach is miserable).

## Feel-Better Soup

SERVES 1 | **Q** | **GF** | **SF**\* | **MA** |

*I call this miso soup "feel-better soup" because it's the one soup I yearn for when I'm sick. You can also extend the servings by cleaning out your fridge. Try adding greens, leftover noodles or rice, cubed tofu, etc. I also like to add 1 tsp of minced fresh ginger for variety.*

- 3  green onions
- 2  c water, divided
- 1  c sliced shiitake mushrooms
     tiny pinch of red pepper flakes
     low-sodium soy sauce\* (optional)
     kelp (optional)
- 1–3  tbsp yellow miso, divided\* (see note)

1. Cut off the rooty bottom of the green onions and discard. Then slice the white and light green parts of the green onions and set aside.
2. Line a medium pot with a thin layer of water.
3. Add mushrooms and sauté over high heat until they start to soften.
4. Add the red pepper flakes and cook for a few seconds.
5. Add onions and remaining water and bring to a near-boil.
6. Once soup is about to start boiling, reduce heat to low.
7. Add soy sauce and kelp (if using) and simmer until thoroughly warm.
8. Add 1 tbsp miso, stirring constantly to prevent clumps.
9. Taste, adding more miso as desired (I usually add a total of 2½ tbsp, but all misos are different).
10. Turn off heat and let rest for 5 minutes, giving the flavors a chance to enhance.

▶▶▶ **CHEF'S NOTE:**

*Since some misos are less salty than others, you may need to add a splash of low-sodium soy sauce, too. If you like your miso soup to have a fish flavor (as it's traditionally served at restaurants), add kelp to taste.*

**Per serving:** 128 calories, 28g fat, 28g carbohydrates, 5.2g fiber, 7.4g sugars, 1.5g protein

# Easter & Passover

My family is Christian and Catholic, but some of our close family friends are Jewish and Greek Orthodox, so Easter/Passover was always a hodge-podge of cultural dishes and foods when I was growing up. (My childhood favorites were deviled eggs [see my version on p. 120] and baklava, in case you were wondering.)

As such, I didn't have a menu (or even a main dish!) in mind when I started thinking about an Easter and Passover section for this book. To keep it universal (and a bit eclectic), I have focused on seasonal ingredients such as asparagus and artichokes, as well as spring-fresh flavors like lemon, garlic, and rosemary.

> For Passover menu ideas see p. 118.
> If your Easter is a little more brunch-like, see the Brunch section on p. 100.
> If you make vegan baklava, please call me and I'll be right over!

Also for parents: You can buy wooden and plastic eggs that dye just like hard-boiled eggs. They're sold at Wal-Mart and other similar retailers, as well as online.

# White Bean Dill Dip

MAKES 1 CUP | **Q** | **GF** | **SF** | **PA** | **P** |

*This is a terrific alternative to hummus. Serve as a party dip, as a crostini topper, or enjoy as a healthy snack with raw vegetables. The lemony-dill flavor makes it perfect for springtime!*

- 1 15-oz can white beans, drained and rinsed
  juice and zest of ½ small lemon (about the size of an egg)
- 1–2 garlic cloves, divided
- 1–1½ tbsp Dijon mustard, divided
  vegetable broth, as needed
- ¼–⅓ c fresh dill, divided
  balsamic vinegar or smoked paprika for garnish

1. In a food processor, combine beans, lemon juice, lemon zest, 1 garlic clove, and 1 tbsp Dijon and whiz until smooth, adding a splash or two vegetable broth if necessary to reach a thick "hummus" consistency.

2. Add 3 tbsp dill and pulse a few times to incorporate.

3. Taste, adding more dill as desired (dill varies in potency based on its freshness), plus more Dijon and/or garlic (if desired), plus a pinch of salt and a few dashes of black pepper. Pulse again.

4. Spoon into the center of a dish, cover with plastic wrap, and chill for 30 minutes or longer if you can (not necessary, but the flavor intensifies). **STOP**

5. Drizzle with balsamic or smoked paprika before serving.

**Per serving (1 tbsp):** 30 calories, 0.2g fat, 5g carbohydrates, 17g fiber, 0g sugars, 2g protein

# Deviled "Eggs"

HOLIDAY HIT

MAKES 12

| **Q** | **GF** | SF | **MA** | P |

*Ann Esselstyn taught me how to make these incredible faux deviled eggs. I added a little black salt to her recipe to give the deviled eggs a more eggy flavor plus a few additional seasonings my mother used in her deviled eggs recipe. I swear, I could eat two dozen of these "eggs" all by myself!*

|       |                                      |
|-------|--------------------------------------|
| 6     | small red potatoes                   |
| ¼     | c hummus (plain)                     |
| 1     | tsp Dijon mustard                    |
| ¼     | tsp garlic powder                    |
| ¼     | tsp onion powder                     |
|       | pinch of black salt                  |
|       | hot sauce (optional)                 |
|       | paprika or smoked paprika for garnish |

1. Boil potatoes until fork-tender, then let cool completely.
2. Meanwhile, mix hummus, Dijon, garlic powder, and onion powder together, plus a pinch of black salt, stirring to combine. (Add hot sauce here if you prefer a spicy deviled egg.) Add more Dijon or black salt to taste, then set aside.
3. Once potatoes cool, slice them in half long-ways and use a little spoon or melon baller to scoop out a small circle of the potato flesh (this is your "egg").
4. Spoon hummus mixture into the hole and garnish with paprika.

▶▶▶ **CHEF'S NOTE:**
*Black salt is also called* kala namak. *Not to be confused with Hawaiian black lava salt.*

**Per "egg":** 69 calories, 0.6g fat, 14.4g carbohydrates, 1.8g fiber, 0.9g sugars, 2.1g protein

---

**VARIATION**
*Deviled Potato Salad: You can also smash up the potatoes (or leftovers) to make a potato salad.*

# Beet Salad

SERVES 2-4 | **Q** | **GF** | SF* | **MA** | P |

*When I was in Finland for the Finnish release of* Everyday Happy Herbivore, *I fell madly in love with a Scandinavian beet salad called* rödbetssallad. *(I visited two vegetarian restaurants on my trip and both offered a vegan version of this exceptional dish.) The beautiful pink color will knock your socks off! To make it a meal, serve over a bed of spinach with chickpeas or white beans.*

|       |                                          |
|-------|------------------------------------------|
| 8     | oz cooked beets, drained                 |
| 2     | tbsp plain vegan yogurt or Vegan Mayo (p. 170)* |
| ¼-½   | tsp Dijon mustard                        |
| 1     | tsp apple cider vinegar                  |
|       | juice of 1 small lemon wedge             |
|       | fresh dill for garnish (optional)        |

1. Chop or slice beets.
2. Mix beets with yogurt (or vegan mayo), mustard, vinegar, and lemon juice (just a touch—a small lemon wedge!), and mix until creamy and pink. Let rest a few minutes and stir again (it'll get creamier).
3. Taste, adding more Dijon, lemon juice, or vinegar if desired. If too tart, add a pinch of sugar or a few drops of agave nectar. Garnish with fresh dill, if using, and serve.

**Per serving (serving 4):** 31 calories, 0.2g fat, 6.2g carbohydrates, 1.1g fiber, 5g sugars, 1.4g protein

# Creamy Grape Salad

SERVES 2-4 | **Q** | **GF** | **SF** | **PA** | **P** |

*This is a beautiful alternative to fruit salad. I love serving this dish at brunch.*

1 c red grapes, sliced
1 c green grapes, sliced
¼ c (or more) plain or vanilla vegan yogurt
brown sugar (optional)
crushed pecan, walnuts, or granola (optional)
dash of cinnamon (optional)

1. Toss grapes with yogurt until covered as desired. (This recipe is pretty flexible. I like a ratio of 2 cups grapes to ¼ cup yogurt, but you might like it more or less creamy.)
2. Chill for at least 30 minutes. **STOP**
3. Top with brown sugar, nuts or granola, and cinnamon, just before serving if desired.

▶▶▶ **CHEF'S NOTES**:
- *For a sweeter salad, whisk sweetener (agave nectar or honey) into your yogurt, or you can drizzle it on top.*
- *If you have leftovers, you can add diced apples, sliced celery, and blueberries, and serve over fresh spinach for lunch.*

**Per serving (serving 2):** 83 calories, 0.7g fat, 17.9g carbohydrates, 0.8g fiber, 17.1g sugars, 2.3g protein

# Potato Salad

SERVES 6 | **Q** | **GF** | **SF\*** | **MA** | **P** |

*This is my family's favorite potato salad. Even before my dad was following a plant-based diet, he was hooked on this dish, and my best friend, Jim, a vegetarian, loves*

*it, too. I take this potato salad to potlucks with great success—even my very omni extended family doesn't miss a beat.*

1 lb red potatoes, cubed or diced
2 tbsp Dijon mustard
⅓ c Vegan Mayo (p. 170)*
¼ c chopped fresh dill
1-2 tsp lemon zest
crumbled vegan bacon (optional)
fresh dill sprigs for garnish (optional)

1. Bring a large pot of water to a boil.
2. Add potatoes and cook until fork-tender.
3. Immediately rinse potatoes with cold water and allow to completely cool.
4. Once room temperature, mix all ingredients, except optional dill sprigs, together in a large bowl.
5. Add pepper to taste if desired.
6. Chill before serving and garnish with fresh dill sprigs, if using.

**Per serving:** 70 calories, 0.4g fat, 15.2g carbohydrates, 1.7g fiber, 1.7g sugars, 2.9g protein

# Savory Glazed Carrots

SERVES 2 | **Q** | **GF** | **SF** |

*These carrots are my go-to side dish. They complement any meal, they come together quickly and easily, and everyone loves them.*

1 tsp cornstarch
2 tbsp water
vegetable broth, as needed
2 tsp Dijon mustard
1 tsp Italian seasoning
¼ tsp pure maple syrup
4 carrots, peeled and chopped

1. Mix cornstarch with cool water into a milky slurry and set aside.

*Savory Glazed Carrots continued...*

2. Line a skillet with a thin layer of broth. Whisk in mustard, Italian seasoning, and maple syrup.
3. Add carrots and bring to a boil over high heat.
4. Reduce to medium and sauté carrots until fork-tender or softer, about 4–5 minutes. Stir regularly and add more broth as needed to prevent sticking.
5. Once carrots are cooked, check liquid, adding more broth as necessary. You want a thin lining of broth on the bottom.
6. Reduce heat to low and stir in cornstarch slurry.
7. Continue to cook, stirring constantly, until liquid thickens into a glaze and coats carrots. Serve warm.

**Per serving:** 72 calories, 12g fat, 15g carbohydrates, 3.6g fiber, 6.8g sugars, 1.4g protein

# Cream of Broccoli Soup

HOLIDAY
HIT

SERVES 2 | **Q** | **GF** | **SF** | **MA** | **P** |

*I like to call this "Use Up Your Leftovers Cream of Broccoli Soup" because your leftover rice or baked potato is the secret "cream" ingredient.*

- 2½ c broccoli (fresh or frozen), divided
- 2–3 c vegetable broth
- 1 small onion, diced
- 1 garlic clove, minced
- ½ c cooked rice or potato, chopped
- 1 c nondairy milk
  basil or thyme (optional)
  nutritional yeast, to taste
  fresh lemon juice (optional)
  red pepper flakes or black pepper for garnish

1. If using fresh broccoli, remove the tough lower stalk but chop the other stalky parts.

2. Line a large pot with vegetable broth and sauté onion and garlic until onion is translucent.
3. Add ½ cup broth and cooked rice or potato and let simmer until rice is waterlogged and extra liquid has all or mostly cooked off; if using potato, cook until potato is very soft and tender. (If using a raw [uncooked] potato, this may take longer and require more liquid than if using a leftover already cooked potato, such as a baked potato from the night before.)
4. If using fresh broccoli, add another ½ cup broth and broccoli, and cook until broccoli is very tender. (Note: If you want a soup with broccoli pieces, scoop some out before they're waterlogged and very soft, and set aside to stir in at the end.)
5. If using frozen broccoli, add broccoli at the end as the rice is finishing up (omit extra ½ cup broth—just a splash will do) or cook briefly in microwave and add to soup with no extra broth.
6. Transfer soup to a blender (or use an immersion blender) and puree with nondairy milk, plus additional broth as necessary to achieve a soup consistency. You can also add fresh or dried basil or thyme, plus salt and pepper to taste here.
7. Return blended soup to your saucepan and let simmer, adding nutritional yeast to taste.
8. Squeeze fresh lemon juice over soup before serving, if desired, and garnish with red pepper flakes or fresh black pepper.

▶▶▶ **CHEF'S NOTE:**

*For a richer soup, blend some raw cashews with water to make a cashew cream and replace the nondairy milk with the cream. To make cashew cream, follow this general rule: 1–2 parts water to 1 part raw cashews (e.g., 2 cups water and 1 cup nuts). If you can, soak your cashews in water overnight before blending. You want a total of 1 cup cream (or thereabouts) for this recipe.*

**Per serving (with rice):** 168 calories, 1.8g fat, 33.9g carbohydrates, 4.4g fiber, 4.3g sugars, 5.7g protein
**Per serving (with potato):** 149 calories, 1.8g fat, 30.3g carbohydrates, 6g fiber, 5g sugars, 5.8g protein

# Lemon-Rosemary Meatballs

MAKES 15 MEATBALLS

| Q | GF* | SF* | MA | P |

*These meatballs just keep popping into my mouth. I love them as an appetizer!*

- 1 small shallot, minced
- 2-3 garlic cloves, minced
- 1 small zucchini, minced
- 1 15-oz can kidney beans, drained and rinsed, mashed well
- 1-2 tbsp lemon zest
- 2 rosemary sprigs, minced
- 2½ tbsp ketchup
- 2½ tbsp steak sauce
- 1 tsp Vegan Worcestershire Sauce (p. 171)*
- ½ c instant oats

1. Combine all ingredients together. Stir well.
2. Roll mixture into walnut-size balls and place on a cookie sheet with parchment paper.
3. Bake at 350°F for 20 minutes or until crispy brown on the outside and pretty firm to the touch.
4. Let cool for 10 minutes. They firm as they cool.

**Per meatball:** 45 calories, 0.5g fat, 8.2g carbohydrates, 1.9g fiber, 16g sugars, 2.3g protein

# Stuffed Artichokes

SERVES 4 | SF | PA | P |

*I'm not going to lie: These artichokes do take a smidgen more work and effort (this a real fancy pants recipe and not a pretend one like all the others in this book), but they're absolutely worth it! Serve with Golden Dressing (p. 173) as a dipping sauce. When I take these to a summer potluck, I feel like I've proven myself as a cookbook author.*

juice of 1 lemon
- 4 artichokes
- 1¼ c vegetable broth plus 3-4 tbsp vegetable broth
- 1 c whole-wheat couscous
- ⅓-½ c minced fresh mint
- ¼-⅓ c minced fresh parsley
- 1 tsp mild curry powder
- 1 tsp onion powder
- 1 tsp garlic powder

1. Fill a large bowl with water and fresh lemon juice and set aside but near your work area.
2. Cut stems off artichokes so they sit flat, then place into the lemon water. One at a time, carefully use a serrated knife to cut off the top third of the artichoke, then use kitchen scissors to clip off and discard sharp leaf points, if any. Place back into the lemon water.
3. Let artichokes soak while you fill a large pot with water, approximately 2 inches deep. Cover and bring to a boil.
4. Once boiling, add artichokes gently, cover, bring to a boil again, then reduce heat to low and steam until tender, about 25–40 minutes. (When the leaves pull out easily and the base is fork-tender, they're cooked.)
5. Drain well and set aside until they're cool enough to handle safely.
6. Meanwhile, bring 1¼ cups vegetable broth (or water) to a boil. Once boiling, immediately add couscous and turn off heat. Couscous will absorb the water in minutes.
7. Fluff couscous with a fork, then add mint, parsley, curry powder, onion powder, and garlic powder, plus a little vegetable broth to help everything incorporate. Stir to combine. Taste, adding more mint or parsley, if desired, plus salt and pepper to taste.
8. Once artichokes are cool, remove the center leaves and scoop out the hairy parts, then discard. STOP
9. Stuff the couscous into the center of the artichokes and in between all the leaves (I won't lie—this makes a mess).

*Stuffed Artichokes continued...*

10. Warm in the oven at 300°F for a few minutes, if desired, and serve.

▶▶▶ **CHEF'S NOTE:**

*Sometimes, instead of boiling and steaming, I pressure-cook my artichokes on high for 1 minute (as recommended by my pressure cooker's user manual). Makes the meal so much easier—and faster, too!*

**Per serving:** 255 calories, 0.8g fat, 54.1g carbohydrates, 12.2g fiber, 2.4g sugars, 11.8g protein

# Mini Soy-Free Quiche

MAKES 12 | **Q** | **GF** | **SF** | **MA** | **P** |

*I never tried quiche until I was plant-based, and from the very first Tofu*

*Quiche (see Tofu Scramble, p. 102) I made, I was smitten. I've come up with all different kinds of flavor combinations over the years, but for this cookbook, I wanted to create a soy-free quiche for those who can't have tofu. Chickpea flour does the trick!*

| | |
|---|---|
| 1 | c chickpea flour |
| 2½ | c vegetable broth |
| 3 | tbsp nutritional yeast |
| 1–2 | tbsp Dijon mustard |
| ½ | tsp black salt (p. 188) |
| 1 | jalapeño, seeded and minced |
| ½ | c cilantro, roughly chopped |
| ½ | c corn (thawed, if using frozen) |
| 1 | c cooked black beans |
| 1 | tomato, diced |

1. Preheat oven to 475°F.

2. Combine chickpea flour, broth, nutritional yeast, Dijon mustard, and black salt in a blender and blend until smooth, creamy, and

frothy. Add remaining ingredients and stir quickly with a spoon (do not blend!). Pour gently into muffin tin.

3. Bake for 10 minutes. Reduce oven temperature to 450°F and bake for another 3–7 minutes or until golden and firm to the touch. Let cool for at least 10 minutes in the pan. (They firm a little as they cool.)

▶▶▶ **CHEF'S NOTES:**

• *I use a nonstick muffin pan and find if I'm patient in letting them cool I can pop them out easily after I run a thin plastic knife closely around the edges. My testers had mixed results with them sticking to a regular metal plan and silicone. Parchment paper cups worked well for everyone.*

• *These quiches store beautifully in the fridge.*

**Per quiche (plain):** 78 calories, 1.5g fat, 11.5g carbohydrates, 3.6g fiber, 1.9g sugars, 5.4g protein

# Carrot Cake Cupcakes

MAKES 12 | **SF** | **MA** | **P** |

*I love carrot cake! This was one of the first recipes I ever posted on happyherbivore.com and it remains one of the most popular. It's a great, crowd-pleasing treat for Easter or a birthday party!*

1½ c whole-wheat pastry flour
1 c raw sugar
1 tsp baking powder
1 tsp baking soda
1½ tsp ground cinnamon
½ tsp fine salt
1½ c unsweetened applesauce
1 generous tsp pure vanilla extract
1 large carrot, peeled and shredded
vegan cream cheese (for icing)
chopped walnuts for garnish
shredded carrot for garnish

1. Preheat oven to 350°F.
2. Line a muffin tin with parchment paper liners or use a nonstick pan.
3. In a medium bowl, whisk together flour, sugar, baking powder, baking soda, cinnamon, and salt.
4. In a large bowl, combine applesauce, vanilla, and carrot.
5. Add dry mixture to wet mixture in 3–4 batches, stirring until just combined.
6. Fill muffin cups ¾ full and bake for 18–25 minutes or until a toothpick inserted into the center comes out clean.
7. Remove cupcakes from oven and transfer to a wire cooling rack.
8. Once the cupcakes are completely cool, slather with vegan cream cheese as an icing, and garnish with walnuts and shredded carrot.

▶▶▶ **CHEF'S NOTE:**

*For a sweeter icing, use electric beaters to mix powdered sugar into the vegan cream cheese (to taste) before icing your cupcakes.*

**Per cupcake (without icing):** 137 calories, 0.3g fat, 32.1g carbohydrates, 2.2g fiber, 20.1g sugars, 1.6g protein

# Picnics, Barbecues & Outdoor Parties

Independence Day, Memorial Day, or just a classic summer barbecue, picnic, or cookout—here's what to make or bring to an outdoor party!

You'll find all your favorites: healthy hot dogs, corndogs, slaws, burgers, sandwiches, and beyond.

I love a good picnic and cookout!

---

**MENU**

### SLAWS, SALADS & BEANS

Cowboy Caviar (p. 54)
Beet Salad (p. 120)
Potato Salad (p. 123) or
  Cajun Potato Salad (p. 62)
Sweet Slaw (p. 132)
Veggie Slaw (p. 132)
Thai Slaw (p. 133)
Cowboy Beans (p. 135)
Baked Beans (p. 135)

"Cheater" Spicy Peanut
  Noodles (p. 136)

### MAIN DISH

Quick Burgers (p. 136)
Smoky Sweet Potato
  Burgers (p. 139)
Kidney Bean–Quinoa
  Burgers (p. 139)
Reuben (p. 140)

pinwheels &
  sandwiches (p. 141)
BBQ Sliders (p. 143)
Carrot Hot Dogs (p. 148)

### GRILL

veggie (& fruit) kabobs (p. 133)

### DRINKS

Sangria (p. 143)
Pink Lemonade (p. 152)

---

# Sweet Slaw

SERVES 4 | **Q** | **GF** | **SF\*** |

*I love this slaw because it comes together as fast as you can chop, and it's really quite stunning. It's a fabulous side dish for four, but also makes a great lunchtime meal for one.*

- ½   small red cabbage
- 1   golden apple
- 1   carrot, peeled
- 1–2   tbsp Vegan Mayo (p. 170)* or vegan yogurt
- ¼   c raisins (optional)

1. Shred or thinly slice cabbage and slice apple and carrot into matchsticks.
2. Mix together with 1 tbsp of vegan mayo or vegan yogurt, making sure everything is evenly coated. Add another ½–1 tbsp of vegan mayo or yogurt if necessary.
3. Sprinkle raisins on top, if using, and serve.

▶▶▶ **CHEF'S NOTE:**
*A little lemon, lime, or orange juice can add a nice citrusy dimension to this slaw.*

**Per serving:** 64 calories, 0.2g fat, 16.5g carbohydrates, 2.7g fiber, 11.8g sugars, 1.1g protein

# Veggie Slaw

SERVES 2 | **GF** | **SF\*** |

*This rustic coleslaw is rich, creamy, and delicious. It goes perfectly on top of salad, spread on crackers, as a side dish to summer meals, or slathered into a veggie sandwich as a condiment.*
*P.S. My husband loves putting it on top of his Carrot Hot Dog (p. 148), along with chili (p. 70 or 72) for a "chili-slaw dog."*

- 1–5   tbsp Vegan Mayo (p. 170)*
-    dash of garlic powder
-    pinch of onion flakes
- ¼   c shredded carrots
- ½   c shredded zucchini

1. Combine mayo with garlic powder and onion flakes, then stir in vegetables.
2. Add salt and pepper to taste. Serve immediately.

**Per serving:** 16 calories, 0.1g fat, 3.5g carbohydrates, 0.7g fiber, 1.7g sugars, 1.0g protein

# Thai Slaw

SERVES 2-3 | **Q** | **GF** | **SF**∗ |

*I love this fiery Thai take on slaw. It really jazzes things up!*

½ head red or white cabbage, thinly sliced
1-2 tbsp Vegan Mayo (p. 170) or plain vegan yogurt∗
few drizzles of rice vinegar
Asian hot sauce (e.g., Sriracha)
few dashes of garlic powder

1. Toss cabbage with mayo or yogurt until it's lightly covered or as creamy as you like (but it will get creamier).
2. Add a few drizzles of vinegar and toss again. Taste, adding more vinegar if desired. (I like my slaws to be pretty vinegary, but my husband likes them sweeter and creamier.)
3. Add a touch of hot sauce (a little Sriracha goes a long way!) and mix.
4. Add several dashes of garlic powder and mix. Taste, adding more heat, garlic, or vinegar if desired.

▶▶▶ **CHEF'S NOTE:**
*Sometimes I squeeze fresh lime juice into this slaw.*

**Per serving:** 48 calories, 1.8g fat, 5.9g carbohydrates, 2.2g fiber, 3.6g sugars, 1.6g protein

## VEGGIE (& FRUIT) KABOBS

You can make veggie kabobs (or fruit kabobs) with grilled vegetables and fruits. Include tofu with peanut sauce, mushrooms, or grilled potatoes to break it up—or even vegan hot dogs! Here are some veggies and fruits that work well for this:

- apples
- asparagus (squeeze lemon juice on it!)
- beets
- carrots
- corn (add chili powder and lime juice, trust me!)
- eggplant
- jalapeños
- onions
- peaches
- pears
- pineapple
- red bell peppers
- Romaine lettuce
- squash (any, especially yellow "summer" squash)

Cowboy Beans

# Cowboy Beans

SERVES 2 | **Q** | **GF** | **SF** | **MA** | **P** |

*Cowboy beans are the rugged relative to baked beans: they're sweet but tangy, and give you a good ol' fashioned kick in the pants with their heat—a nice Southwest twist! These quick and easy beans are a great addition to any summer barbecue menu and they're easy enough to make at a campfire, too!*

|      | vegetable broth, as needed |
|------|---------------------------|
| 1    | medium onion, diced |
| 3–5  | garlic cloves, minced |
| 1    | tsp chili powder |
| 2    | tbsp ketchup |
| 2    | tbsp smoky barbecue sauce |
| 1    | tsp prepared yellow mustard |
| ½–1  | tsp Dijon mustard |
| 1    | 15-oz can pinto beans, drained and rinsed |
| ¼–½  | tsp smoked paprika |
| ¼    | tsp pure maple syrup |
|      | cayenne pepper or hot sauce (optional) |
|      | brown sugar (optional) |
|      | pickled jalapeño slices for garnish (optional) |

1. Line a large skillet with a thin layer of vegetable broth. Sauté onion and garlic until onion is translucent.
2. Add chili powder, stirring to coat onions and garlic. Stir in ketchup, barbecue sauce, yellow mustard, and Dijon mustard.
3. Add in beans and stir to combine. Gently warm over low for a few minutes. Add smoked paprika and maple syrup.
4. Stir again and taste, adding more Dijon, barbecue sauce, or cayenne or hot sauce, if using, as desired.
5. Cover and simmer over low heat until the flavors blend together. For a sweeter dish, add brown sugar (or more maple syrup) to taste, plus a splash of broth if necessary.
6. Garnish with pickled jalapeño slices if using and serve with cooked greens and cornbread or rice. I also like these beans (and regular baked beans) over sweet potatoes.

▶▶▶ **CHEF'S NOTE:**
*A popular addition is a bell pepper (seeded and diced), which you can include for some color. Cook it with the onions and garlic.*

**Per serving:** 258 calories, 2.4g fat, 49.8g carbohydrates, 12.2g fiber, 10.6g sugars, 12.1g protein

# Baked Beans

SERVES 4

| **Q** | **GF\*** | **SF\*** | **MA** | **P** |

*It's not a summer get-together or family barbecue without baked beans, and these are my family's favorite. In fact, my parents love them so much that they always make a double batch, substituting kidney beans for the second can of navy beans.*

|      |  |
|------|--|
| ½    | small onion, diced |
| 1    | garlic clove, minced |
| 1    | 15-oz can navy beans, drained but unrinsed |
| 2    | tbsp ketchup |
| 2    | tbsp molasses |
| 1    | tsp Dijon mustard |
| 1    | tbsp low-sodium soy sauce\* |
| 2–3  | tbsp pure maple syrup |
|      | light dash of cayenne pepper |

1. Preheat oven to 300°F.
2. Cook onion and garlic in ¼ cup water over high heat until the onion is translucent, about 2 minutes.
3. Add remaining ingredients and bring to a boil.
4. Once boiling, remove from heat and transfer mixture to a casserole dish, cover with foil, and bake for 30 minutes.
5. Let rest for 15 minutes, allowing the sauce to thicken.

*Baked Beans continued...*

6. Stir to incorporate before serving.

▶▶▶ **CHEF'S NOTE:**

*If your beans come out soupy, you can transfer them to a saucepan and cook them uncovered over high heat for a few minutes to reduce the liquid.*

**Per serving:** 160 calories. 0.1g fat. 33.9g carbohydrates. 6.0g fiber. 13.7g sugars. 6.3g protein

# Quick Burgers

MAKES 4 | **Q** | **GF** | **SF** | **PA** | **P** |

*This is my go-to quick bean burger! It's embarrassing how often I make it, but it's so easy and so fast!*

- 1 15-oz can black beans, drained and rinsed
- 2 tbsp ketchup
- 1 tbsp prepared yellow mustard
- 1 tsp onion powder
- 1 tsp garlic powder
- ⅓ c instant oats

1. Preheat oven to 400°F.
2. Line a cookie sheet with parchment paper and set aside.
3. In a mixing bowl, mash black beans with a fork until mostly pureed but with some half beans and bean parts left.
4. Stir in condiments and spices until well combined, **STOP** then mix in oats.
5. Divide into 4 equal portions and shape into thin patties.
6. Bake for 10 minutes, carefully flip over, and bake for another 5 minutes, or until crusty on the outside.
7. Slap onto a bun with extra condiments and eat!

**Per burger:** 109 calories. 0.5g fat. 17.6g carbohydrates. 3g fiber. 2.2g sugars. 5g protein

# "Cheater" Spicy Peanut Noodles

SERVES 1 | **Q** | **GF**∗ | **SF**∗ | **PA** | **P** |

*This recipe comes from my 7-Day Meal Plan service (getmealplans.com). Peanut noodles are a quick and easy meal I picked up in college (just peanut butter on hot noodles!) but now I've lightened the load with vegan yogurt, and I've added a few nice garnishes to make it feel more upscale. It's a super quick and easy weeknight meal and potluck favorite!*

- 4 oz noodles∗
- 2 tbsp plain vegan yogurt
- 1 tbsp peanut butter
- 1 tbsp low-sodium soy sauce∗
  Asian hot sauce (e.g., Sriracha), to taste
  bean sprouts for garnish (optional)
  green onions, sliced, for garnish (optional)

1. Cook noodles according to package instructions, drain, and rinse with cold water. **STOP**
2. While the noodles cook, whisk yogurt with peanut butter and soy sauce (reduce if your peanut butter is salty) and hot sauce to taste (I like it *hot*, with 1–2 tsp).
3. Garnish with bean sprouts and green onions, if desired, and serve.

▶▶▶ **CHEF'S NOTE:**

*This recipe doubles beautifully.*

**Per serving:** 282 calories. 10.8g fat. 35.4g carbohydrates. 2.5g fiber. 4.4g sugars. 11.8g protein

Smoky Sweet Potato Burgers

# Smoky Sweet Potato Burgers

MAKES 5 | **Q** | **GF** | **SF** | **PA** | **P** |

*I love a good bean burger, but sweet potato burgers are in a category of their own! These smoky-sweet but spicy burgers will dazzle anyone they're served to, so if your friends tend to snub bean burgers and other faux meats, try serving these at your party. They're so beautiful guests can't help to be intrigued . . . then wowed!*

- 1 **15-oz can white beans, drained and rinsed (see note)**
- 1 **c mashed sweet potato**
- 1 **tbsp nutritional yeast**
- 1¼ **tsp smoked paprika**
- 1 **tsp onion powder**
- 1 **tsp garlic powder**
- 1 **tsp ground cumin**
  **few drops of liquid smoke (about ½ tsp)**
- 2-3 **tbsp ketchup**
- ⅓ **c rolled oats**
- ¼ **c instant oats**
  **hot sauce, to taste (optional)**
  **chipotle powder, to taste**

1. Preheat oven to 400°F. Line a cookie sheet with parchment paper and set aside.
2. Mash beans with fork or pulse in a food processor so no whole beans are left, but it's still chunky with some half beans. Mix with mashed sweet potato, nutritional yeast, spices, liquid smoke, and ketchup (use 3 tbsp for a slight tomato flavor), stirring to combine. **STOP**
3. Add all oats and stir to combine again. Add hot sauce if desired, plus a few dashes of chipotle powder (to taste—a little goes a long way!), plus salt and pepper if desired. Taste, adding more heat or smoke as desired.
4. Pick off 5 equal-sized portions and roll into balls with damp hands. Place balls on cookie

sheet (leaving room to spread) and smash lightly with your palm into patties.
5. Bake for 10 minutes (patties should be somewhat firm after 10 minutes; if not, wait a few more minutes), flip with a spatula, and bake for 5 more minutes. Then flip again and bake for another 2–5 minutes, until deep in color, crisp, and firmer, but careful not to burn.

▶▶▶ **CHEF'S NOTES:**
- *Two small sweet potatoes (or 1 large) should make 1 cup mashed sweet potato. I cook mine in the microwave, then mash and mixed with nondairy milk (about 2 tbsp) to make "mashed potatoes." I leave my potato skins on for added nutrition, but you can peel them off after cooking, if desired.*
- *Any canned white bean (e.g., navy) will work in this recipe.*

**Per burger:** 177 calories, 0.9g fat, 34.7g carbohydrates, 7.4g fiber, 4.6g sugars, 8.3g protein

# Kidney Bean- Quinoa Burgers

MAKES 6 | **GF\*** | **SF\*** | **P** |

*I find kidney beans lend themselves better to a true "burger" flavor and have a better consistency. Serve these burgers on a whole-wheat bun with all the fixin's.*

- ¼ **c quinoa**
- 1 **15-oz can kidney beans, drained and rinsed**
- 2 **tbsp barbecue sauce**
- 2 **tbsp ketchup**
- 2 **tbsp low-sodium soy sauce\***
- 1 **tbsp prepared yellow mustard**
- 1 **tsp onion powder**
- 1 **tsp garlic powder**
- 1 **tbsp Italian seasoning**
- ½ **tsp paprika**
- ⅓ **c vital wheat gluten\* (see note)**

*Kidney Bean–Quinoa Burgers continued...*

1. In a small saucepan, combine quinoa with ½ cup water, cover, and bring to a boil.

2. Once boiling, reduce heat to low and continue to cook until fluffy and all the water has evaporated, about 15 minutes.

3. Meanwhile, mash beans with a fork in a mixing bowl until they have the consistency of refried beans.

4. Add remaining ingredients in order, plus cooked quinoa, and stir to combine.

5. Preheat oven to 450°F and line a cookie sheet with parchment paper.

6. Break mixture into 6 equal segments. Roll each into a ball, flatten it, and shape it into a patty using your hands.

7. Bake for 8 minutes, flip, and bake for 8 more minutes, then flip again for 5 minutes, but only if necessary. When the burgers are brown and crisp on the outside, they are done.

▶▶▶ **CHEF'S NOTE:**

*For gluten-free, substitute Orgran's Gluten Free Gluten Substitute for the vital wheat gluten.*

**Per burger:** 316 calories, 2.1g fat, 53.7g carbohydrates, 11.6g fiber, 4.6g sugars, 22.4g protein

# Reuben

SERVES 1 | **Q** | **GF*** | **SF*** | **PA** |

*My husband has been after me to create a healthy, vegan version of the Reuben sandwich for as long as he's been plant-based. I kept resisting, wondering how I'd re-create corned beef. "Why not try portobellos?" he asked. His suggestion was spot on. It's amazing how much these portobellos taste (and look!) like corned*

*beef. When I was working on the recipe, my in-laws were visiting and my mother-in-law could not believe how much it looked like beef—all the way to the pink coloring!*

```
1    very large portobello mushroom
1    tbsp low-sodium soy sauce*
1    tbsp nutritional yeast
½    tsp onion powder
½    tsp garlic powder
½    tsp ground ginger
1    c water
1    tbsp red wine vinegar
     few dashes of ground cinnamon
     few dashes of ground allspice or cloves
½–¾  tsp fennel seeds
½    tsp Vegan Worcestershire Sauce (p. 171)*
2    slices of rye bread (or other)
     sauerkraut, as desired
     Rémoulade Sauce (p. 53)
```

1. Remove woody stem from mushroom and slice into chunky strips, and down the middle, for long strips that are 2–3 inches long.

2. Whisk soy sauce, nutritional yeast, onion powder, garlic powder, and ginger with water.

3. Whisk in vinegar, 1–2 light dashes of cinnamon, 1–2 very light dashes of allspice or cloves, and black pepper as desired (depends on how peppery you like "beef").

4. Pour half of the mixture into a skillet and add mushrooms and fennel seeds. Sauté for a few minutes.

5. When the liquid has reduced, add the rest of the soy sauce–water mixture, stir in Worcestershire sauce, cover, and sauté for a few minutes longer, until the liquid has really reduced and the mushroom strips are a dark brown. (They should be softer, but not really soft or mushy—barely tender and firm.) **STOP**

6. Place on top of toasted rye, spooning juices over top. Add sauerkraut, rémoulade (it tastes a lot like Thousand Island dressing, which is traditionally used), and you're done!

**Per serving (just mushroom component):** 86 calories, 0.8g fat, 13g carbohydrates, 4.4g fiber, 1.7g sugars, 9.1g protein

# PINWHEELS & SANDWICHES

## Pinwheels

Pinwheels make sandwiches a cute finger food. They're easy to make and the options are limited only by your imagination. (P.S. Kids love pinwheels!)

To make a pinwheel with sandwich bread, remove the crusts and flatten with a rolling pin (rolling once, or twice, max). Add toppings on each slice of bread and roll up. Stick 3 toothpicks into the roll (to hold it closed) and slice into 3 sections. If using a tortilla or wrap, skip the flattening step.

PB&J or just jam or jelly (red varieties are really stunning!), hummus and spinach, and shaved carrots with raisins and vegan yogurt or cream cheese are popular pinwheel flavors with kids.

"Tuna" Salad (p. 50) and hummus with shredded veggies like red cabbage, carrots, onion, bell pepper, olives, and/or spinach are popular with adults.

My go-to party pinwheel wrap: arugula, black beans, and Chipotle Aioli (p. 78).

Use wrap recipes in my other cookbooks and meal plans for more ideas!

## Party Sandwiches

Sandwich rings are an old party standby, and while supermarket delis and sandwich shops like Subway will generally make vegetable-only sandwich platters for you, you'll have more options with homemade sandwiches. If you're pressed for an easy fix, get the platter but offer an array of condiments (including hummus or several hummus flavors) so your guests can jazz up their sandwiches. Piles of faux deli meats or vegan cheese slices so guests can add those to the vegetable sandwiches are another option.

## Tea Party Sandwiches

Tea party sandwiches are regular sandwiches that have the crusts removed and are cut into small triangles or squares—but that makes them fancy, see? You can also use cool cookie-cutter shapes to make heart- or flower-shaped sandwiches, which add a nice touch for a ladies lunch or bridal shower. (If your little princess is having a birthday tea party, these fancy pants sandwiches are a must!) For variety, use several different types of bread, including white, wheat, rye, and pumpernickel.

The same flavor suggestions for pinwheels apply here, plus I also like to use the crab cake mixture (Crab Cakes with Rémoulade Sauce, p. 53) for a seafood sandwich; White Bean Dill Dip (p. 118) as a spread; and cucumbers with vegan cream cheese for a classic tea sandwich.

Beautifully garnished Crostini (p. 49) also work!

## Meatball Subs

Meatball subs are my favorite party buffet option! Buy hot dog buns and keep your meatballs in marinara sauce (No-Meat Meatballs, p. 91, and store-bought marinara for ease) in a slow cooker on low. Guests can assemble the subs themselves.

# BBQ Sliders

SERVES 8 | **Q** | **GF\*** | **SF** |

*Here's my healthy alternative to pulled-pork sliders. A common replacement in vegan circles is jackfruit, but I find it's pretty hard to come by, and cabbage is more my speed anyway. Keep in mind with dishes like pulled pork, or even hot wings, we're typically going gaga for the sauce more than anything, so as long as you use a barbecue sauce you love, and the texture is close enough, you're in business! I love using my Cola Barbecue Sauce (p. 172) in this recipe.*

|       |                            |
|-------|----------------------------|
| ½     | head cabbage               |
|       | vegetable broth, as needed |
| ¼–½   | c barbecue sauce           |
| 8     | whole-wheat buns or other  |

GARNISHES
Dill pickle slices (optional)
caramelized onions (optional) (see note)

1. Remove core and outer green part from cabbage. Discard or save for homemade vegetable broth. Slice white parts very thinly into long strands.
2. Line a large pot with a very thin layer of broth. Add sliced cabbage and cook over high, stirring constantly with tongs and incorporating until softer, but *not* very soft or flimsy, about 2 minutes (think pulled-pork consistency).
3. Drain off any remaining liquid, then stir in ¼ cup barbecue sauce. Stir to coat, adding more sauce as necessary. (I tend to add about 6 tbsp, but I like my sliders wet and messy!)
4. Pile into bun with onions and pickles if using.

▶▶▶ **CHEF'S NOTE:**

*For caramelized onions, cook sliced onion in a thin layer of vegetable broth until golden and translucent, in as little liquid as necessary, or bake until golden and crisp.*

**Per serving (without bun, using ¼ c sauce):** 23 calories, 0.1g fat, 5.4g carbohydrates, 1.2g fiber, 3.5g sugars, 0.6g protein

# Sangria

SERVES 8 | **Q** | **GF** | **SF** | **MA** | **P** |

*My love for sangria knows no bounds. On my last trip to Barcelona, I watched a bartender make a pitcher of sangria, and carefully jotted down everything he used. This is the result. It's strong but delicious and perfect for parties.*

|   |                                      |
|---|--------------------------------------|
| 2 | bottles cheap and fruity red wine    |
| 1 | c orange-flavored vodka (see note)   |
|   | juice of 1 orange                    |
| 4 | c seltzer water (see note)           |
| 1 | cinnamon stick (optional)            |
| 2 | apples, sliced                       |

1. In a large pitcher, mix wine, vodka, orange juice, and seltzer, stirring to combine.
2. Add cinnamon stick and sliced apples, if desired.
3. Chill for several hours, then serve over ice.

▶▶▶ **CHEF'S NOTES:**
- *Any orange-flavored liquor can be used in place of the vodka.*
- *Any fizzy water can be used in place of seltzer. Sprite or 7Up might also work.*

**Per serving:** 243 calories, 0.1g fat, 12g carbohydrates, 1.1g fiber, 6.7g sugars, 0.3g protein

## VARIATION

*Sangria Spritzer: For a lightened-up take on sangria, fill a punch bowl with large ice cubes, orange slices, apple slices, and 1–2 cinnamon sticks. Squeeze juice from another orange into the bowl. Add chilled red wine and mixed-berry-flavored sparkling water as desired.*

# Kid-Approved Parties

I get a lot of requests to write a "kid-friendly" cookbook, but the trouble is you can't really write one with recipes that would get a thumbs-up from *all* kiddos. Every kid is so different, with varying levels of pickiness, and kids tend to go through phases, too. (What they loved on Monday, they now hate on Thursday!) Even my nieces and nephews from the same two parents never seem to agree on anything. Some of that might be sibling rivalry at play, but it sure doesn't make mealtime any less dramatic. Still, I know there are a few foods that most kids tend to like, so for this cookbook, I created some healthy dishes that you can serve at your kids' parties with confidence.

## MENU

**LIGHT SNACKS**

fruit kabobs (p. 133)
PB&J Muffins (p. 146)
Soft Pretzels (p. 159)

**PASTA**

Baked Mac Bites (p. 52)
Homemade
  Spaghetti-Ohs (p. 147)

**SOUPS**

Cream of Broccoli Soup (p. 124)
Tomato Soup (p. 147)
Chickpea Noodle Soup (p. 151)

**MAIN DISH**

Meatloaf Bites (p. 51)
Quick Burgers (p. 136)
Grilled Cheeze (p. 148)
Carrot Hot Dogs (p. 148)
Mini Corndog Bites (p. 151)

**DESSERTS**

Chocolate Chip Cookies
  (p. 80)
Ninny's Fruit Spring
Rolls (p. 152)
Vanilla Birthday
Cupcakes (p. 159)

2-Ingredient Cookies (p. 160)
Banana "Cake" Pops (p. 160)

**DRINKS, SHAKES & SMOOTHIES**

Pink Lemonade (p. 152)
Apple Jack Shake (p. 155)
Caramel Cream Shake (p. 155)
Creamsicle Smoothie (p. 155)
Chocolate Shake (p. 156)
Peanut Butter Cup Shake
  (p. 156)
Mint Chocolate Shake (p. 156)

# PB&J Muffins

MAKES 12 | **SF** | **MA** | **P** |

*Childhood's favorite sandwich has been turned into a portable muffin. My testers' kids and grandkids went bonkers for these muffins!*

      2  c white whole-wheat flour
      1  tbsp baking powder
      ½  tsp fine salt
      ¼  c brown sugar
      1  ripe banana
 ¼–½  c peanut butter
      5  tbsp applesauce
      1  c nondairy milk
      ½  tsp pure vanilla extract
     12  tsp (¼ c) jelly, divided

1. Preheat oven to 350°F. Line muffin tin with paper or silicone cups or use a nonstick pan, and set aside.
2. Whisk flour, baking powder, and salt together. Stir in sugar.
3. In a blender, combine banana, ¼ cup peanut butter, applesauce, nondairy milk, and vanilla extract, and blend until smooth and creamy.
4. Pour wet mixture into dry mixture and stir. If it's too dry (all peanut butters are a little different), add more applesauce. Taste, adding more peanut butter if desired (I like just a light flavor, but a strong flavor would need more).
5. Scoop a spoonful and fill each muffin cup so the bottom half is covered (use about half of the batter for 12 muffin cups).
6. Spoon 1 tsp jelly on top of each portion. Then top with a spoonful of batter, covering the jelly. (Make sure jelly doesn't peek out.)
7. Bake for 18–25 minutes (mine are usually done at exactly 20½ minutes). Use a toothpick to test the top of the muffin, but don't go all the way or you'll hit jelly!

**Per muffin (with ¼ c peanut butter):** 153 calories, 3.1g fat, 28.2g carbohydrates, 1.4g fiber, 8.5g sugars, 3.7g protein

# Homemade Spaghetti-Ohs

SERVES 4 | **Q** | **GF\*** | **SF** | **MA** | **P** |

*Ask my mom: I never ate SpaghettiOs as a kid, but I know I'm the exception. Most people loved 'em and now you have a healthy, plant-based version for your kiddos—or for yourself if you need a trip down memory lane! This recipe comes from fellow Herbie Andrea Ferek!*

| | |
|---|---|
| 1 | 15-oz can plain tomato sauce |
| 15 | oz nondairy milk |
| 1 | tsp garlic powder |
| 1 | tsp onion powder |
| ½ | tsp paprika |
| ¼ | tsp salt |
| 1–2 | tbsp nutritional yeast (optional) |
| 1 | 7-oz pkg O-shaped pasta\* |
| | ketchup, to taste (optional) |
| | pinch of sugar (optional) |

1. Stir tomato sauce, nondairy milk (Andrea says, "Use the empty tomato sauce can to measure the milk"), plus spices and nutritional yeast together in a medium saucepan.
2. Bring the tomato mixture to a boil and stir in the pasta.
3. Turn the heat down to low and cook pasta as it simmers, stirring often to keep the pasta from sticking to the bottom of the pan. Continue to cook and stir the mixture until the pasta is tender. (The time will vary depending on the size and shape of the pasta, so check your package.)
4. Add splashes of water as necessary to keep the sauce from becoming too dry.
5. Once pasta is cooked, taste and adjust seasonings. Add a squirt of ketchup or a pinch of sugar if you prefer your sauce on the sweeter side.

**Per serving:** 196 calories, 2.6g fat, 35.6g carbohydrates, 2.9g fiber, 4.9g sugars, 8.8g protein

# Tomato Soup

SERVES 6 | **Q** | **GF** | **SF** | **MA** | **P** |

*I love serving this simple tomato soup with Grilled Cheeze (p. 148)—perfect for dunking!*

| | |
|---|---|
| 1 | 14-oz can whole, peeled plum tomatoes |
| 2 | c vegetable broth |
| 1 | tbsp onion flakes |
| | dash of garlic powder |
| 2 | tsp Italian seasoning, or to taste |
| 1 | bay leaf |
| 1 | tbsp white vinegar |
| 5–10 | baby carrots, minced |
| | dash of red pepper flakes |
| 1 | tsp mild curry powder |
| 1–2 | tbsp raw sugar or 1–2 tsp agave nectar, as needed |
| | AJ's Vegan Parmesan (optional, p. 172) |

1. Carefully drain the tomato sauce from the can into a large soup pot.
2. Carefully remove each tomato and gently squeeze its liquids into the pot.
3. Pull the whole tomatoes apart into bite-size pieces and toss in.
4. Add vegetable broth, onion flakes, garlic powder, Italian seasoning, bay leaf, vinegar, carrots, red pepper flakes, and curry powder, stirring to combine.
5. Cover and bring to a boil, then reduce heat to low and let simmer for 25 minutes.
6. If the soup is too acidic, add raw sugar or agave as needed. Continue to cook for 5 more minutes.
7. Remove bay leaf and add salt, pepper, and vegan Parmesan to taste.

**Per serving:** 52 calories, 0.5g fat, 11.8g carbohydrates, 1.8g fiber, 5.6g sugars, 1.6g protein

# Grilled Cheeze

MAKES 2 SANDWICHES | **Q** | **GF\*** | **SF** |

*This "cheese" sauce is ooey, gooey, and spreads thickly, really capturing that grilled-cheese consistency. I love to dunk my grilled cheese into a bowl of Tomato Soup (p. 147) or eat it alongside a garden salad.*

⅓ c nutritional yeast
½ c nondairy milk
2 tbsp white whole-wheat flour\*
2 tbsp cornstarch
1 tbsp ketchup
2 tsp prepared yellow mustard
1 tsp onion powder
1 tsp garlic powder
¼ tsp dried dill
4 slices of toast

1. Whisk all the ingredients through dill together in a saucepan and heat over high heat, stirring constantly until really thick. (It will get lumpy then thick.)
2. Smear "cheese" on toast and serve.

**Per serving (without bread):** 185 calories, 1.8g fat, 31.3g carbohydrates, 7.5g fiber, 5.9g sugars, 15.3g protein

# Carrot Hot Dogs

SERVES 2 | **GF\*** | **SF\*** | **MA** | **P** |

*Yves makes an oil-free vegan hot dog, but I still wanted something a little more wholesome for my nieces and nephews. Ann Esselstyn turned me on to the idea of making hot dogs out of carrots, which sounds weird, I know, but works strangely well. You won't believe how much they smell (and taste!) like hot dogs!*

2 carrots, peeled and each end trimmed
1 tbsp low-sodium soy sauce\*
2 tbsp vegetable broth
1 tbsp rice vinegar
½ tbsp apple cider vinegar
1 tsp prepared yellow mustard
  dash of allspice or cloves
  dash of ground nutmeg
  dash of smoked paprika
  dash of cayenne pepper
½ tsp onion powder
½ tsp garlic powder
  drop or two of liquid smoke

1. Line a pot with a layer of water and steam or boil carrots until fork-tender (think hot dog texture) but don't overcook. You don't want your carrots to get too soft or they'll feel soggy.
2. Meanwhile, dump remaining ingredients into a resealable plastic bag.
3. Add carrots. Seal and marinate for at least 24 hours (48 is better).
4. Transfer carrots and marinade to a skillet and simmer in juices until carrots are warm and most or all of the marinade has evaporated. Serve.

**Per carrot dog:** 43 calories, 0.3g fat, 7.7g carbohydrates, 1.9g fiber, 3.5g sugars, 1.6g protein

# Mini Corndog Bites

HOLIDAY HIT

MAKES 18 | Q | GF* | SF* | MA | P |

*So easy, so good, and so darn cute for a party. Kiddos love 'em!*

- 2½ vegan hot dogs*
- ½ c yellow cornmeal
- ½ c white whole-wheat flour*
- 1½ tsp baking powder
- 1 tsp onion powder
- 1 tsp garlic powder
- ¼ tsp paprika
- ¼ tsp dry mustard
- dash of black pepper
- dash of dried oregano (optional)
- cayenne pepper, to taste (optional)
- pinch of fine salt
- 1½ tbsp pure maple syrup
- 2 tbsp unsweetened applesauce
- ¼–½ c nondairy milk

1. Cut vegan hot dogs into 1-inch pieces.
2. Preheat oven to 400°F. Set aside nonstick mini muffin tin (must be mini).
3. Whisk dry ingredients together, then add maple syrup, applesauce, and ¼ cup nondairy milk. You want a thick, pancake-like batter.
4. Spoon 1 tbsp of mixture into each muffin cup. Press hot dog piece into center. Bake for 8–10 minutes or until golden and firm to the touch.
5. Run knife around edges, then wait a few minutes before lifting out. Serve with mustard!

**Per bite:** 36 calories, 0.3g fat, 7.1g carbohydrates, 0.7g fiber, 1.4g sugars, 1.7g protein

# Chickpea Noodle Soup

SERVES 4 | Q | GF* | SF* | MA | P |

*This soup is a favorite of my parents and my best friend, Jim. I crave it when I'm sick.*

- 8 c vegetable broth, divided
- 3 carrots, peeled and sliced
- 2 celery stalks, sliced
- 1 small onion, diced
- 8 oz brown mushrooms, bottoms removed and sliced
- 1 tsp miso (yellow, white, or chickpea)
- 1 tsp low-sodium soy sauce*
- 4 oz noodles or pasta (any shape)*
- 1 15-oz can chickpeas, drained and rinsed

1. Line a large soup pot with broth. Add carrots, celery, and onion and sauté over high heat until onion is translucent, about 3 minutes.
2. Add mushrooms and more broth if necessary.
3. Continue to cook over high heat until the mushrooms are soft, about 3 minutes.
4. Add remaining broth and soy sauce. Cover and bring to a boil.
5. Once boiling, add pasta and reduce heat to medium. Cook for another 6 minutes or until pasta is al dente (check your package and adjust time accordingly).
6. Stir in chickpeas and add miso to taste. Add more salt if necessary or desired.

**Per serving:** 373 calories, 5g fat, 69.3g carbohydrates, 9.5g fiber, 11.9g sugars, 16.2g protein

# Pink Lemonade

SERVES 2 | **Q** | **GF** |

*This recipe came to me by way of my friend Chef AJ, who adapted a recipe she learned at a blender demonstration. It's the best pink lemonade I've ever had and it's made strictly from fruit—no sugar!*

    1  small lemon
    1  c frozen red grapes
    1  c fresh red grapes

1. Zest and juice lemon into a blender.
2. Add frozen and fresh grapes, plus ¼ cup cold water, and blend, adding another ¼ cup water if necessary (add enough water so it blends together).
3. Taste, adding more grapes if it's too tangy.

**Per serving:** 67 calories, 0.3g fat, 17.8g carbohydrates, 0.9g fiber, 15.5g sugars, 0.7g protein

# Ninny's Fruit Spring Rolls

MAKES 12 ROLLS | **Q** | **GF** | **SF\*** | **MA** | **P** |

*This recipe visits from* Happy Herbivore Abroad. *Pair with melted chocolate or peanut butter.*

    ½  lb firm tofu (optional)*
    1  banana
    ½  apple
    12  spring roll wrappers
    2  large strawberries, chopped
       agave nectar (optional)

    **DIPPING SAUCE**
    1–2  tbsp peanut butter or vegan chocolate
       chips
    ¼  c nondairy milk

1. Press tofu, then cut block into 4 slabs. Cut each slab into 3 pieces, for a total of 12 sticks.
2. Cut banana in half, then slice halves lengthwise. Next, slice each quarter into 3 strips, for a total of 12 banana slices.
3. Slice half an apple into ⅛- to ¼-inch-wide strips.
4. Fill a deep dish, large pot or pan with about ¼ inch of water—enough water to cover 1 wrapper. Place 1 spring roll wrapper in cold water for 30–40 seconds (or according to package directions). If the wrapper is not soaked long enough, it is difficult to wrap, and if it is soaked for too long, it can easily tear. Gently take the wrapper out of water dish and let excess water drip off.
5. Place wrapper on a flat surface. Place 1 stick of tofu if using, and 1 slice of banana in the center of the wrapper, then add a few slices of strawberry and apple. Drizzle agave on top, if using.
6. Pick up the bottom of the wrapper and fold over the fillings, pick up one side and fold it over, then repeat with the other side. Roll wrapper all the way to the top. Repeat with remaining ingredients.
7. To make the dipping sauce, warm 1–2 tbsp peanut butter or melt vegan chocolate chips in the microwave, then whisk in nondairy milk as necessary to achieve a sauce consistency (you may need to reheat).

▶▶▶ **CHEF'S NOTE:**

*Courtney says, "I place the wrapper on a cutting board with the bottom hanging off of the board. This makes it easier to pick the wrapper up and roll it."*

**Per roll (with tofu, without dipping sauce):** 120 calories, 1.3g fat, 22.4g carbohydrates, 1.2g fiber, 2.2g sugars, 4.8g protein

# Apple Jack Shake

SERVES 1 | **Q** | **GF** | **SF** |

*Kids love this green smoothie that tastes exactly like the cereal it's named after.*

- 1 c nondairy milk
- 1 frozen banana
- 1 date (or 1 tbsp raisins)
- ½ red apple, chopped
- 1 c fresh spinach
- ¼ tsp ground cinnamon

1. Combine all ingredients except cinnamon in a blender and whiz until smooth. If you don't have a powerful blender, you might want to soak the date or raisins overnight.
2. Add more milk as necessary.
3. Add a few dashes of cinnamon and serve.

**Per serving:** 213 calories, 3g fat, 47.9g carbohydrates, 7.6g fiber, 29.2g sugars, 3.4g protein

# Caramel Cream Shake

SERVES 1 | **Q** | **GF** | **SF** |

*This smoothie is rich and creamy with a subtle hint of cinnamon and caramel. Kids love it! It's also hugely popular with my 7-Day Meal Plan users (getmealplans.com).*

- 1 frozen banana
- 1 c nondairy milk
- 1–2 dates (see note)
- ¼ tsp pure vanilla extract (optional)
- ¼–½ tsp ground cinnamon (optional)

1. For best results, soak dates in hot water first to soften them up a bit for best blending.
2. Combine all ingredients in a blender and whiz until smooth.

▶▶▶ **CHEF'S NOTE:**
*You can substitute ¼–½ tsp (or to taste) agave nectar or maple syrup for the dates.*

**Per serving:** 192 calories, 3.5g fat, 41.4g carbohydrates, 22g fiber, 24.9g sugars, 2.7g protein

# Creamsicle Smoothie

SERVES 1 | **Q** | **GF** | **SF** |

*This shake has all the flavors of the kid-favorite push-up pop! (At least, the push-up popsicles were my favorite!)*

- 1 c orange juice (about 2 oranges) orange zest (optional)
- 4 ice cubes
- ¾ c nondairy milk
- ¼ tsp pure vanilla extract (optional) agave nectar or honey to taste (optional)

1. Combine all ingredients in a blender and blend until smooth and creamy.
2. Taste, adding more zest and/or vanilla extract, and agave nectar or honey if desired.

**Per serving:** 147 calories, 3.1g fat, 27.9g carbohydrates, 1.5g fiber, 21g sugars, 2.5g protein

# Chocolate Shake

SERVES 1 | **Q** | **GF** | **SF** |

*A few years ago I had a pretty severe case of food poisoning and could only sip on liquids. This was one of the smoothies I never tired of and I find kids love it, too—completely unaware they're eating greens! We call this a "Chocolate Green Goddess" on the 7-Day Meal Plans (getmealplans.com).*

> 1   c cold water
> 2-3 dates
> 1   frozen banana
> 2   c fresh spinach
> 2-3 tbsp unsweetened cocoa
>     ice (optional)

1. Combine all ingredients in a blender and whiz until smooth.
2. Taste, adding more cocoa if desired.

▶▶▶ **CHEF'S NOTE:**

*I find this smoothie is best super cold, so I add an ice cube or two.*

**Per serving:** 225 calories, 2.5g fat, 56.6g carbohydrates, 11.6g fiber, 30.3g sugars, 6.4g protein

# Peanut Butter Cup Shake

HOLIDAY HIT

SERVES 1 | **Q** | **GF** | **SF** |

*What kid doesn't love a peanut butter cup? After I shared this recipe in* Everyday Happy Herbivore, *dozens of mamas e-mailed me to say how much their kids loved this shake as an after-school or after-practice treat. (P.S. Big kids love it, too!)*

> 2   frozen bananas
> 1   tbsp smooth peanut butter
> 1   tbsp unsweetened cocoa
> ¼   c nondairy milk

1. Combine all ingredients in a blender.
2. Whiz until smooth, adding more nondairy milk as necessary.

**Per serving:** 334 calories, 10.1g fat, 65g carbohydrates, 9g fiber, 31.9g sugars, 9.1g protein

# Mint Chocolate Shake

SERVES 1 | **Q** | **GF** | **SF** |

*Perfect for St. Patrick's Day and all year long!*

> 1   c unsweetened almond milk
> 1   banana, frozen
> 1   c fresh spinach, packed
> ¼   c fresh mint—about 1 sprig (or mint extract— just a drop or two)
>     chocolate syrup (optional)
>     vegan chocolate, crushed (optional)
> 1   date (optional, for a sweeter shake)

1. Drizzle syrup in your serving glass, if using.
2. In a blender, combine almond milk with banana, spinach, mint, date (if using) and ice cubes (if desired) and blend until smooth and green. Pour into prepared glass and top with crushed chocolate, if desired.

**Per serving (without optional ingredients):** 152 calories, 2.8g fat, 30.9g carbohydrates, 6.7g fiber, 14.2g sugar, 3.8g protein

# Soft Pretzels

MAKES 8 | SF | MA | P |

*I have always loved* (loved!) *soft pretzels. Maybe it's the fond memory I have as a child eating them in New York City, or maybe, as my husband says, they're just a vehicle for getting more mustard into my mouth. (I love mustard—especially spicy and grainy German mustards with my pretzels!) Whatever the reason, I love them, and now I can have a healthier, whole-wheat version in my own home. (They also come in handy at my annual Oktoberfest party!)*

- 2½ c white whole-wheat flour
- 1 tsp agave nectar or sugar
- 1 active yeast packet
- pinch of salt
- 1 c warm water
- 1 tsp baking soda
- 1 c lukewarm water
- coarse salt or cinnamon-sugar for sprinkling

1. Put flour in a mixing bowl and create a well.
2. In another bowl, add agave and yeast, and slowly stir in warm water ("hot" water from the tap is usually just right) so it dissolves and is cloudy. You don't want boiling hot water, however.
3. Pour mixture into flour. Stir until you can't, then use your hands. Once you have a dough, knead. Keep kneading until it's smooth and tacky but not sticky. Put in a plastic bag, seal, and set aside for about 30 minutes.
4. Preheat oven to 425°F.
5. Your dough should have doubled and look like it's about to pop the bag. If it hasn't expanded (risen is the technical term), give it a few more minutes. If it still doesn't rise, your yeast is dead—time to start over. (Super hot water can kill your yeast).
6. Place dough on a floured surface and cut into 8 equal pieces. Roll each into a long rope, then shape each into a pretzel. Place pretzels on a cookie sheet lined with parchment paper.
7. Mix baking soda with lukewarm water. Wet fingers and apply to each pretzel (wet the pretzel with the water on your fingers) and sprinkle with salt or cinnamon-sugar.
8. Bake for 8–10 minutes, until golden and firm to the touch. Then broil for 30 seconds to 1 minute to get that nice outer coating.

**Per pretzel:** 130 calories, 0.7g fat, 27.1g carbohydrates, 3.9g fiber, 1.8g sugars, 5.3g protein

# Vanilla Birthday Cupcakes

SERVES 12 | SF | MA | P |

*These cupcakes are perfect for parties. I also use the dry ingredients in this recipe as a basic cake mix. For example, try using it with a can of pineapple, a can of pumpkin, or a can of soda—all those old semi-homemade tricks we used to love.*

- 2 c whole-wheat pastry flour
- 1 tsp baking powder
- ½ tsp baking soda
- ½ tsp fine salt
- ¼ c applesauce
- ½ to 1 c raw sugar
- 1 c nondairy milk
- 1 tsp lemon extract or zest
- 1 recipe Vanilla Icing (p. 170)

1. Preheat oven to 350°F.
2. Line a muffin tin with parchment paper liners or use a nonstick pan.
3. In a medium bowl, whisk flour, baking powder, baking soda, and salt together.

*Vanilla Birthday Cupcakes continued...*

4. In a large bowl, whisk applesauce, sugar, nondairy milk, and lemon extract or zest until well combined.

5. Pour dry mixture into the wet mixture in 3–4 batches, stirring until just combined.

6. Spoon batter into muffin cups ¾ full and bake for 15–25 minutes or until a toothpick inserted in the center comes out clean.

7. Transfer to a wire cooling rack.

8. Once the cupcakes have fully cooled, slather icing over top and serve.

▶▶▶ **CHEF'S NOTE:**

*This recipe also works for making a regular-size cake if you bake it longer.*

**Per cupcake (no icing, 1 c sugar):** 144 calories, 0.4g fat, 33.5g carbohydrates, 0.7g fiber, 17.3g sugars, 2.2g protein
**Per cupcake (½ c sugar):** 113 calories, 0.4g fat, 25.1g carbohydrates, 0.7g fiber, 8.9g sugars, 2.2g protein

# 2-Ingredient Cookies

MAKES 12–18 | **Q** | **GF** | **SF** | **MA** | **P** |

*These cookies need no introduction. The name says it all!*

    2    very ripe bananas
  1½–2  c rolled oats
    ¼    c chocolate chips, raisins, or other add-ins
         ground cinnamon, to taste (optional)
         ground cardamom, to taste (optional)

1. Mash bananas really well with a fork or potato masher until paste-like.

2. Stir in 1½ cups rolled oats, add-ins, and spices, if using. Stir (it'll get wetter as you stir). If it's really wet or sticky, add more oats. (You need to be able to handle it. Any more than 2 cups oats would probably make too dry a cookie, though.)

3. Using clean hands, pick off walnut-sized pieces, roll in balls, then use your palm to flatten each cookie to 2 × 2 inches.

4. Bake on parchment-lined cookie sheet or Silpat mat at 350°F for 8–15 minutes or until cookies are firm enough to pick up (they harden more as they cool).

**Per cookie (serving 12, 1½ c oats, no add-ins):** 56 calories, 0.7g fat, 11.4g carbohydrates, 1.6g fiber, 0.4g sugars, 1.5g protein

# Banana "Cake" Pops

SERVINGS VARY | **Q** | **GF** | **SF** |

*A healthy alternative to cake pops! I highly recommend having a do-it-yourself banana pop station at your child's next birthday party. Or make it a fun play date group activity! Even adults get into it!*

         bananas
         melted chocolate (p. 98)
         vegan marshmallows (optional)

    **TOPPINGS**
         crushed nuts
         sprinkles
         crushed cookies
         crushed graham crackers (s'mores on a stick!)
         mini chocolate chips
         crushed espresso beans (for adults)
         coconut flakes

1. Peel bananas and cut into the desired size.

2. Skewer each onto a stick.

3. Coat banana in melted chocolate and dip in toppings of choice.

▶▶▶ **CHEF'S NOTE:**

*I find super ripe bananas (while tasty) tend to slide. Placing a vegan marshmallow (or part of one) on both ends of the banana on the stick helps hold it in place.*

**Nutritional information for this recipe varies widely.**

# LARGE (& MIXED) CROWD ENTERTAINING

## Party Bars

When you need to feed a large crowd, party bars are a fuss-free and trendy way to go. Party bars are also the perfect solution when you're trying to entertain both omnivores *and* vegetarians. Each guest gets to customize his or her own meal, which means you can accommodate any kind of special diet or taste preference, *no problemo*!

# Taco Bar

taco "meat"*

lettuce

tomato

onions

Vegan Sour Cream (p. 171)

pico de gallo

rice

refried beans

taco shells/nacho chips/Adobo Tostados (p. 76)

Quick Queso Sauce from Nachos Grande
  (p. 76) or commercial vegan cheese

guacamole/avocado

black beans

salsa

cabbage

pineapple salsa

Portobello Steaks (p. 86)

*To make your own, see Lentil Taco Meat, Happy
  Herbivore Abroad, p. 43.

# Hot Dog Bar

Perfect during summer barbecues! You can find vegan
hot dogs at most stores (even Target and Walmart)
for an easy buffet, or make your own Carrot Hot Dogs
(p. 148).

## TOPPINGS:

ketchup

mustard (variety)

relish

chili

vegan cheese

Veggie Slaw (p. 132)

Thai Slaw (p. 133)

Sweet Slaw (p. 132)

Vegan Mayo (p. 170)

peperoncini

jalapeño (pickled)

pickles (slices and long spears)

banana peppers

sauerkraut

red bell peppers (roasted, in water not oil)

onions (red and white)

caramelized onions (p. 143)

green bell peppers

tomatoes ("dragged-through-the-garden"
  style!)

celery salt

salsa/pico de gallo

Rémoulade Sauce (p. 53)

oyster crackers

barbecue sauce

hot sauce

vegan cream cheese (Seattle style)

cabbage

Sriracha

pinto beans

vegan bacon

guacamole

salsa verde

crushed corn chips

Tip: You can do a "hamburger" bar, too—serving
up commercial veggie burgers like Boca burgers
or homemade burgers, such as Quick Burgers
(p. 136).

# Oatmeal Bar

Perfect for business conferences, outdoor events, and big brunch parties, an oatmeal bar is a fuss-free, healthy, and budget-friendly way to tackle breakfast for a large crowd.

Cook the oatmeal ahead and keep it warm in a slow cooker or pressure cooker (using the "warm" setting). Depending on your slow cooker or pressure cooker, you might even be able to cook the oatmeal directly in it. (This also makes oatmeal very easy for transport if you're having an off-site picnic or event.)

P.S. Muffin tins make great trays for holding all the different toppings!

### TOPPINGS:

peanut butter

almond butter

sliced bananas

blueberries

brown sugar

pure maple syrup (or honey)

nuts (peanuts, pecans, walnuts)

raisins

chocolate chips (for kids!)

▶▶▶ CHEF'S NOTE:

*Most catering services offer the oatmeal option. Tell them you only want oats and water—no butter or milk mixed in.*

# Sweet Potato Bar

Sweet potato bars are a lot of fun when you're camping or any time you want an easier breakfast bar.

You'll need sweet potatoes (pre-baked in foil), of course, plus a variety of toppings!

### TOPPINGS:

vegan yogurt

applesauce

dried fruit

pecans

peanuts

peanut butter

cinnamon

pure maple syrup

pumpkin pie spice

bananas

chocolate

# Waffle Bar

Waffles (p. 105) are a lot of fun with kids for sleepovers (mostly because kids turn the waffles into a makeshift sundae).

### TOPPINGS:

sliced strawberries

sliced bananas

Coconut Whipped
  Cream (p. 98)

melted chocolate

chocolate syrup

powdered sugar

blueberry sauce

pecans

walnuts

sprinkles

peaches

blueberries

raspberries

blackberries

chocolate chips

# Breakfast Taco Bar

You can also turn your taco bar (p. 164) into a breakfast or brunch taco bar by adding steamed kale, Tofu Scramble (p. 102), and sweet potatoes to the menu and lineup. Everyone loves a breakfast burrito!

Another option (kids love this!) is breakfast nachos. Pile warmed refried beans (or black beans) on corn chips, with salsa, guacamole, Tofu Scramble (p. 102; optional), green onion, and a sprinkling of nutritional yeast or vegan cheese. You can also put all this goodness over a baked potato (or baked sweet potato) and crumble the corn chips over top.

# Broths, Sauces, Seasonings & More 🐘

# No-Chicken Broth

MAKES 1 CUP  | Q | GF | SF | MA | P |

*This is my DIY version for faux chicken broth powder. To make broth, mix 1 tbsp of the powder into 1 cup of warm or hot water.*

- 1⅓ c nutritional yeast
- 2 tbsp onion powder
- 1 tbsp garlic powder
- 1 tsp dried thyme
- 1 tsp rubbed sage (*not* powdered)
- 1 tsp paprika
- ½ tsp turmeric
- ¼ tsp celery seed
- ¼ tsp dried parsley

Combine all ingredients in a mortar and pestle, then grind into a fine powder.

**Per serving (1 tbsp):** 12 calories, 0.1g fat, 1.7g carbohydrates, 0.7g fiber, 0g sugars, 1.3g protein

# No-Beef Broth

MAKES 1 CUP  | Q | GF* | SF* | MA | P |

*This is my DIY version for faux beef broth and it can easily be made gluten- and soy-free.*

- 1 tbsp low-sodium soy sauce*
- 1 tbsp nutritional yeast
- ½ tsp Vegan Worcestershire Sauce (p. 171)*

- ¼ tsp onion powder
- ¼ tsp garlic powder
- ¼ tsp ground ginger
- ⅛ tsp pepper

1. In a medium saucepan, whisk all ingredients together with 1 cup of water until well combined.
2. Bring to a boil and let simmer for 1 minute.
3. If you used water and low-sodium soy sauce, you might want to add a little salt.

▶▶▶ **CHEF'S NOTE:**
*If you use this broth in a soup recipe, add a bay leaf during cooking.*

**Per serving (1 c):** 27 calories, 0.2g fat, 4.3g carbohydrates, 1.1g fiber, 0.7g sugars, 2.7g protein

# Vegetable Broth

MAKES 4 CUPS  | GF | SF* | MA |

*Nothing beats the ease of premade broth or bouillon cubes, but homemade vegetable broth is superior in comparison. It's also a great way to use up veggies that are on their way to expiration or leftover veggie parts like broccoli stems, onion peels, or carrot shavings. (There's a video on happyherbivore.com of me making "leftovers" broth in my pressure cooker.)*

```
1    onion (any), peeled
1    large carrot
1    celery stalk
3-4  garlic cloves, peeled
1-2  tsp yellow miso* (see note)
4    whole peppercorns
1    bay leaf
     fresh or dried herbs (any)
     plus any three of the following:
     1    small brown potato
     2-4  small red potatoes
     1    c mushrooms
     1    bell pepper, seeded
     1    medium turnip
     1    medium zucchini
     1    parsnip
     1    leek
```

1. Transfer your selections to a large pot. If using dried herbs, grab each green one you have on hand and give it a good shake into the pot. Otherwise, add about 3–5 oz fresh dill, but any complementary fresh herbs on hand will do.

2. Add 1 tsp of miso or salt, black peppercorns, and bay leaf.

3. Add 8 cups cold water, or 10 cups water if your selections are particularly big.

4. Cover and bring to a boil. Reduce heat to low and simmer until the vegetables are falling apart, about 1 hour.

5. Turn off heat and allow to cool to a warm temperature.

6. Use tongs or a spoon to remove bay leaf and vegetables.

7. Grab a cheesecloth or fine strainer and strain liquid into a plastic container.

8. Cool to room temperature, then store in the fridge for up to 3 days. After 3 days, store in freezer in 1-cup measurements.

▶▶▶ **CHEF'S NOTE:**

*You can omit the miso and add salt to taste for a soy-free vegetable broth.*

**Per serving (1 c):** 49 calories, 0.4g fat, 10.6g carbohydrates, 2.2g fiber, 4.1g sugars, 2.2g protein

# Whole-Wheat Pizza Dough

SERVES 8 | **SF** | **MA** |

*Pizza goes gourmet, too! To make artisan pizza, go cheeseless with a medley of wild mushrooms (fresh parsley to garnish). Other rich combinations (like butternut and tofu ricotta) can also make "pizza" feel a little sophisticated. Call it a tart or galette if you want to feel fancy pants!*

```
1    pkg active yeast
1    c warm water
1    c whole-wheat flour
2    c whole-wheat pastry flour
3    tbsp vital wheat gluten
1    tsp salt
1    tbsp raw sugar
1    tbsp yellow cornmeal
```

1. Stir yeast in warm water and let sit for 5 minutes or until the water is a beige color.

2. Meanwhile, combine flours, wheat gluten, salt, and sugar.

3. Make a well in center of your dry ingredients, pour yeast mixture in, and stir until it forms a ball of dough.

4. Turn out onto a clean surface, lightly floured with cornmeal, and knead for 5 minutes. The dough should be a smooth, elastic ball.

5. Place in a glass or metal bowl and cover. Put it in a warm place, such as an unheated oven, and wait for it to double in size. It will take about an hour of resting for the dough to rise sufficiently. (If your dough does not rise, your yeast is dead and you'll have to start over. Too hot water can kill your yeast.)

6. Punch the dough, reshape into a ball, and let it rise again.

7. Freeze or refrigerate if not using immediately (do not refrigerate for more than 24 hours).

*Whole-Wheat Pizza Dough continued . . .*

8. When ready to use, divide into 1, 2, or 4 equal portions and roll into a pizza shape. Add toppings and place on pizza stone, pizza pan, or cookie sheet lined with parchment paper.

9. Bake for 5–10 minutes at 450°F.

▶▶▶ **CHEF'S NOTE:**

*Double or triple this recipe when you are making it and store leftovers in the freezer so you always have healthy whole-wheat pizza dough on hand.*

**Per serving:** 173 calories, 0.7g fat, 35.5g carbohydrates, 3.4g fiber, 16g sugars, 4.6g protein

# Tofu Yogurt

SERVES 2 | **GF** |

*This DIY version is much more economical than commercial vegan yogurts.*

- 1 12.3-oz pkg Mori-Nu tofu (any firmness)
- 1 cold banana (see note)
- 2 tbsp nondairy milk
- 2 tbsp fresh lemon juice
- 2 tbsp sweetener (optional)

1. Combine tofu, banana, nondairy milk, and lemon juice in a blender or food processor and whiz until smooth and creamy.

2. Taste, adding sweetener such as pure maple syrup or agave nectar to taste if desired. I like to leave the yogurt unsweetened (it reminds me of Greek yogurt) and drizzle with agave nectar over top.

▶▶▶ **CHEF'S NOTES:**

- *Add fresh or frozen fruit (such as strawberries or blueberries), ¼ cup at a time, for fruit-flavored yogurts.*
- *Bananas turn brown when they oxidize, meaning the yogurt will turn brown if you make it ahead and leave it in the fridge. It hasn't gone bad; it just doesn't look pretty. If you do a fruit flavor, however, you usually can't notice the color change. You can*

*also blend without the banana and reblend with the banana before serving to keep the color white.*

**Per serving (unsweetened):** 128 calories, 1.4g fat, 17.3g carbohydrates, 1.6g fiber, 9.1g sugars, 13.4g protein
**Per serving (sweetened):** 192 calories, 1.4g fat, 34.6g carbohydrates, 1.6g fiber, 26.3g sugars, 13.5g protein

# Vanilla Icing

SERVES 12 | **Q** | **GF** | **SF** | **MA** |

*Classics never go out of style. Mmm, icing!*

- 1 c powdered sugar
- 1 tbsp nondairy milk
- 1 tsp vanilla extract
  food coloring (optional)

1. Stir ingredients together to combine.

2. Add more sugar to thicken the icing or more nondairy milk to thin it out. Ideally, you want the consistency to be a paste-like glaze.

3. Add food coloring, if desired.

**Per serving (2 tbsp):** 40 calories, 0g fat, 10g carbohydrates, 0g fiber, 9.8g sugars, 0g protein

# Vegan Mayo

MAKES 1 CUP | **Q** | **GF** | **MA** |

*Some generic low-fat mayos (such as Trader Joe's brand) are accidentally vegan, but no commercial vegan mayo is totally oil-free anymore. I make my own mayo from tofu, but in a pinch vegan yogurt (same amount) with a touch of lemon or white vinegar does the trick. Vegenaise also makes a soy-free mayo for those needing to avoid soy, though it contains oil.*

- 1 12.3-oz pkg Mori-Nu tofu
- 2–3 tbsp Dijon mustard
- 2 tsp distilled white vinegar
  fresh lemon juice, to taste
  agave nectar, to taste

1. In a blender or small food processor, blend tofu with Dijon and vinegar until smooth and creamy.
2. Add a few drops of lemon juice and a few drops of agave nectar and blend again.
3. Taste and add more lemon, agave, or Dijon as needed or desired. Chill until you're ready to use.

▶▶▶ **CHEF'S NOTE:**

*How long this mayo lasts depends on how fresh the tofu was when you bought it, as well as your fridge and climate. It should last you at least a week, and tofu usually turns pink and smells awful when it goes bad. Regrettably, you cannot freeze tofu-based mayo, so plan a few recipes around it when you make a big batch.*

**Per serving (1 tbsp):** 9 calories, 0.2g fat, 0.3g carbohydrates, 0g fiber, 0g sugars, 1.6g protein

# Vegan Sour Cream

MAKES 1 CUP | **Q** | **GF** |

*Quick and easy and so healthy!*

| | |
|---|---|
| 1 | 12.3-oz pkg Mori-Nu firm tofu |
| 2–4 | tbsp fresh lemon juice |
| ½ | tsp distilled white vinegar |
| ⅛ | tsp fine salt |
| 1 | tsp dry mustard powder |
| | agave nectar, to taste |
| | light dash of garlic powder |
| 1 | tsp dried or fresh dill (optional) |

1. Combine tofu with 2 tbsp lemon juice, vinegar, a pinch of salt, mustard powder, a few drops of agave, and a light dash of garlic powder and blend until smooth and creamy.
2. Taste and add more lemon and/or sweetener if necessary or desired. Stir in dill before serving if using.

**Per serving (1 tbsp):** 13 calories, 0.2g fat, 1.4g carbohydrates, 1.1g sugars, 1.6g protein

**VARIATION**
*Lime Crème: Use lime juice instead of lemon juice and add 1½ tbsp chopped fresh cilantro.*

# Vegan Worcestershire Sauce

MAKES 1 CUP | **GF\*** | **SF\*** | **MA** | **P** |

*Most commercial Worcestershire sauces contain anchovies, although there are a few vegetarian brands on the market. While nothing beats the ease of bottled sauce, this DIY recipe is allergen-free and very inexpensive to make.*

| | |
|---|---|
| 6 | tbsp apple cider vinegar |
| 2 | tbsp low-sodium soy sauce* |
| 1 | tbsp brown sugar or 1 tsp molasses (*not* blackstrap) |
| 2 | tsp prepared mustard (any) |
| ¼ | tsp onion powder |
| ¼ | tsp garlic powder |
| ¼ | tsp ground cinnamon |
| | light dash of cayenne pepper or chili powder |
| | light dash of allspice or ground cloves |
| ¼ | c water |

1. Whisk all ingredients together with water until well combined.
2. Add salt if desired.
3. Store in an airtight container in the fridge.

**Per serving (1 tsp):** 2 calories, 0g fat, 0.4g carbohydrates, 0g fiber, 0g sugars, 0.1g protein

# Cola Barbecue Sauce

MAKES 2¼ CUPS | **Q** | **GF\*** | **SF\*** | **MA** | **P** |

*THIS IS THE BEST BARBECUE SAUCE I'VE EVER HAD! (All caps necessary!) It's so easy and ridiculously addictive, too. Take it to summer parties and show off! You're fancy pants with homemade sauce!*

|     | vegetable broth, as needed |
| --- | --- |
| 1 | small onion, minced |
| 2 | garlic cloves, minced |
| 12 | oz cola |
| 2–4 | tbsp ketchup |
| 6 | oz can tomato paste |
| 2 | tbsp prepared yellow mustard or Dijon mustard |
|  | light dash or two allspice or cloves |
| 1 | tsp Vegan Worcestershire Sauce (p. 171)\* |
| 1 | tsp smoked paprika |
|  | bay leaf |
|  | cayenne pepper or hot sauce, to taste |
|  | browning sauce, as needed |
| 2–3 | drops liquid smoke |

1. Line a large pot with a thin layer of broth and sauté onion and garlic until translucent and liquid has evaporated.
2. Add remaining ingredients, whisking to combine.
3. Cover and heat over low for 10–20 minutes, until it reduces and gets darker in color. If it's not reducing, cook longer and leave lid slightly ajar.
4. Taste, adding more ketchup (this will vary based on the sweetness of the cola you use), cloves, liquid smoke, or heat as desired.
5. For a more vinegary taste, add apple cider vinegar or red wine vinegar. For sweeter, add brown sugar. To darken the color, add browning sauce—just a little!

▸▸▸ **CHEF'S NOTE:**

*My testers tried this sauce with a number of different colas: Coke, Pepsi, diet, natural, and so forth. Despite the taste differences everyone loved "their version," so go with any soft drink you prefer.*

**Per serving (2 tbsp, with diet soda):** 14 calories, 0.1g fat, 3g carbohydrates, 0.6g fiber, 1.7g sugars, 0.6g protein
**Per serving (2 tbsp, with regular soda):** 20 calories, 0.1g fat, 4.7g carbohydrates, 0.6g fiber, 3.4g sugars, 0.6g protein

# AJ's Vegan Parmesan

MAKES 1½ CUPS | **Q** | **GF** | **SF** | **MA** |

*If you can't find commercial vegan Parmesan where you live, here is a great alternative recipe by my friend Chef AJ. AJ says, "I've made this with almonds, walnuts, cashews, even Brazil nuts. For those with a nut allergy, use sesame seeds."*

| 1 | c nuts |
| --- | --- |
| ½ | c nutritional yeast (see note) |
|  | pinch of salt or salt-free seasoning (optional) |

1. Put nuts and nutritional yeast in a blender.
2. Add salt or other seasoning if desired.
3. Process until a smooth powder has formed.
4. Store in an airtight container in the fridge for up to a week.

▸▸▸ **CHEF'S NOTE:**

*You can also start with less nutritional yeast (3–4 tbsp), adding more to taste.*

**Per serving (1 tbsp, with cashews):** 45 calories, 2.8g fat, 3.4g carbohydrates, 1g fiber, 0g sugars, 2.4g protein

# Golden Dressing

MAKES ABOUT ½ CUP

| Q | GF | SF* | MA | P |

*This recipe visits us from Happy Herbivore Light & Lean and is my favorite dressing to serve. My omni friends practically drink it, they love it so much. Add more miso for a miso dressing, more Dijon for a spicy or tangy dressing, more lemon for a lemony dressing, and so on. I also like to substitute peanut butter or tahini for the miso on occasion.*

    ¼   c cold water
    ¼   c nutritional yeast
    1-2 tbsp Dijon mustard
    1   tbsp pure maple syrup or 1-2 dates
    ½   lemon, skin removed and seeded
    1   tbsp yellow miso* (see note)

1. Combine all ingredients in a blender and blend until smooth and creamy, adding more water if you like a thinner dressing (note: this dressing thickens as it chills in the fridge).
2. Taste, adding more nutritional yeast, Dijon, maple syrup, lemon, or miso as desired.

▶▶▶ **CHEF'S NOTE:**
*I use yellow miso, but white, red, or chickpea miso should also work. Do not use brown miso.*

**Per serving (1 tsp, with miso):** 21 calories, 0.3g fat, 3.3g carbohydrates, 1g fiber, 1.2g sugars, 1.8g protein
**Per serving (1 tsp, with peanut butter):** 25 calories, 0.9g fat, 3.2g carbohydrates, 1g fiber, 1.2g sugars, 1.9g protein

# Cajun Seasoning

MAKES ½ CUP   | Q | GF | SF | MA |

*I prefer blending my own Cajun seasoning since some brands can be explosive in terms of heat. If you prefer to use a commercial blend for convenience, I like McCormick Gourmet Collection Cajun Seasoning and Badia Louisiana Cajun Seasoning.*

    2   tbsp sweet paprika
    2   tbsp garlic powder
    1   tbsp cayenne pepper
    1   tbsp chili powder
    1   tbsp pepper
    1   tbsp dried oregano or marjoram
    1   tbsp onion powder
    ½   tsp ground nutmeg or mace (optional)

1. Combine all spices and herbs thoroughly.
2. Store in an airtight container.

**Per serving (1 tbsp):** 24 calories, 0.6g fat, 4.9g carbohydrates, 1.9g fiber, 0g sugars, 1.1g protein

# Creamy Cajun Mustard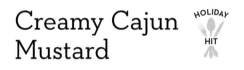

MAKES ⅓ CUP   | Q | GF* | SF* | MA |

*You can find commercial creamy Cajun mustard in Louisiana, but I love homemade best!*

    3   tbsp Dijon mustard
    ½   tsp Vegan Worcestershire Sauce (p. 171)*
    ½   tsp hot sauce
    1   tsp molasses
    1   tbsp Vegan Mayo (p. 170) or plain vegan yogurt*
    ¼   tsp Cajun Seasoning (p. 173)

1. Combine all ingredients, adding more Cajun Seasoning if you like.
2. If your Dijon is too strong, you can add a bit more mayo to tone it down. You can also add a touch more molasses for a sweeter mustard.

**Per serving (1 tbsp):** 12 calories, 0.4g fat, 1.8g carbohydrates, 0g fiber, 1.1g sugars, 0.6g protein

# Appendix

## HOLIDAY FAQS

Here are the most frequent questions about the holidays I get from fans.

### I'm the only veghead—what do I do?

I always (always!) recommend telling hosts about your dietary restrictions beforehand. You may think it's more considerate to keep quiet, to ensure that the host goes to no extra trouble. But I had a heartbreaking experience once where I said nothing at all, showed up, and the host ended up crying. She felt so bad that there was nothing for me to eat. I kept insisting it was fine, I was fine, but alas. I felt terrible for days.

Ease the situation by offering to bring your own plate or a dish everyone can try, and tell them you'll make your main meal, such as the Thanksgiving Menu for One or Two (p. 12).

Also try working with your host to see if a tiny tweak can make a traditional recipe suitable for you. For example, maybe they cook with vegetable broth instead of chicken broth.

### Should I talk about my diet/beliefs?

In my opinion, Thanksgiving (or any major holiday) is not the best time to bring it up. It's one thing if someone is curious, or asks a question—by all means answer them; but most people don't want to hear how meat and dairy clogs their arteries and feeds cancer after they've just eaten those very foods (or are about to) . . . *ya know*?

Emotions (and stress) tend to run a little high during holidays, too, and you don't want an argument to break out. Nor do you want to be *that* person.

Leading by example and being compassionately quiet goes a long way in these circumstances.

## What if I get picked on? Or someone instigates an argument with me?

First, remind yourself why they are being hostile. It's not really about you—it's about them. You've rocked the boat. You've challenged the status quo and they fiercely want to protect it. In essence, you've become a mirror. Your choices have made them reflect back on themselves, and they don't like what they see. They respond by attacking you to make themselves feel better.

Second (and this is important!) keep your cool. Don't let them get a rise out of you. End the conversation by saying, "I prefer not to talk about this right now, but I can send you some articles/websites later if you'd like to know more."

You're not going to change their mind that day, in that conversation, so don't waste your energy or emotions.

## Seeing them eat animal foods makes me sad. How can I cope?

Remind yourself that you were once one of them. Most of us were not raised plant-based. Most of us were confused and misguided about what is healthy (or what is not healthy). Most of us have been duped by marketing and mainstream noise (even if it hurts to admit it). Most of us thought vegan or plant-based sounded extreme, until we were motivated to try it and realized it wasn't so extreme after all.

Our friends and loved ones don't know what we do, or they know and they're not ready, or they know and they don't give a hoot.

This is not always easy, but you have to pick your battles. The journey you're on is about you, not them.

Be kind. Stay compassionate. Educate and lead by example. Realize that you could be the person that changes their life—just not on Thanksgiving!

## Should I cave this once for family peace?

Doing so only makes the situation worse in the long run.

One of my fans gave this advice to another newer Herbie, and it's spot-on:

> As long as you give in, compromise, or do anything contrary to what you are saying you believe, you are just reinforcing the idea that you are not really serious about this and can easily be swayed or bullied into what they want you to do. Just be kind but firm. Do not budge one inch or you will never be taken seriously and the harassment will never stop.

## How do you deal with "Oh come on, it's a special day ... cheat!" situations?

Explain that you don't feel you are missing out, and you're not there for the food. You're there for the family, love, gratitude, and memories. You don't go to a wedding for a cake; you go to be in the presence of love and watch a loved one marry the love of their life.

A great diffuser is "I'm all good, thanks ... but you enjoy" or even "I don't feel like I'm missing out and if I do eat that, I'll be cheating on my goals for myself, and I'd rather not do that."

Although it's not the most diplomatic approach, you can also turn it back on them. I had one family member that was just relentless, so I finally asked point-blank, "Why is it so important to you that I eat this? Why is it so important to you that I cheat?" They left me alone after that.

# MORE HOLIDAY RECIPES

I've given you menus and recipes for a dozen occasions throughout the year, but here are some additional recipes from my other books that you might want to try if you need more dishes or would like to try something different.

## THANKSGIVING

Lentil Loaf
  (*Happy Herbivore Abroad*, p. 257)
Peppered Mushroom Gravy
  (*Happy Herbivore Abroad*, p. 262)
Golden Scallion Gravy
  (*Happy Herbivore Abroad*, p. 263)
Pumpkin Pancakes
  (*Happy Herbivore Light & Lean*, p. 20)
Harvest Salad
  (*Happy Herbivore Light & Lean*, p. 133)
Sweet Kale Salad
  (*Happy Herbivore Light & Lean*, p. 180)
Spice Cake Surprise
  (*Happy Herbivore Light & Lean*, p. 223)
Glazed Pumpkin Biscuits
  (*Everyday Happy Herbivore*, p. 57)
Harvest Cornbread
  (*Everyday Happy Herbivore*, p. 65)
Tempeh Meatloaf
  (*Everyday Happy Herbivore*, p. 180)

Sage Gravy
(*Everyday Happy Herbivore*, p. 288)
Corn Pudding
(*The Happy Herbivore Cookbook*, p. 173)
Torkey (Tofu Turkey)
(*The Happy Herbivore Cookbook*, p. 152)

Want even more options for your Thanksgiving menu? I put a huge blog post together every November on happyherbivore.com/topic/Holiday with a long list of 50-plus recipes that make for a perfect plant-based Thanksgiving. It's the perfect place to go if you need more ideas for more plant-based dishes for the big day. You can also click the "Holiday" tab on the blog for more ideas all year long!

## WINTER HOLIDAYS

Swedish Split Pea Soup
(*Happy Herbivore Abroad*, p. 24)
"Cheater" African Green Beans
(*Happy Herbivore Abroad*, p. 73)
Pesto-Stuffed Mushrooms
(*Happy Herbivore Abroad*, p. 99)
Moroccan Vegetables
(*Happy Herbivore Abroad*, p. 105)
Insalata Fantasia
(*Happy Herbivore Abroad*, p. 111)
Almond Cookies
(*Happy Herbivore Abroad*, p. 148)
Bread Pudding
(*Happy Herbivore Abroad*, p. 156)
Lentil Loaf
(*Happy Herbivore Abroad*, p. 257)
Winter Confetti Salad
(*Happy Herbivore Abroad*, p. 267)
Ruby Chocolate Muffins
(*Happy Herbivore Light & Lean*, p. 41)
Carol's Cabbage Soup
(*Happy Herbivore Light & Lean*, p. 107)
Lentil & Pear Salad
(*Happy Herbivore Light & Lean*, p. 128)
Skinny Mac 'n' Cheese
(*Happy Herbivore Light & Lean*, p. 150)
Lentil Marinara Sauce
(*Happy Herbivore Light & Lean*, p. 155)
Molasses Cake
(*Happy Herbivore Light & Lean*, p. 221)
Mint Mocha
(*Happy Herbivore Light & Lean*, p. 254)
Chai-Oat Cookies
(*Everyday Happy Herbivore*, p. 246)
Gingerbread Mini-Loaves
(*The Happy Herbivore Cookbook*, p. 51)
African Kale and Yam Soup
(*The Happy Herbivore Cookbook*, p. 64)
Baked Tofu Parmesan
(*The Happy Herbivore Cookbook*, p. 139)
Baked Ziti
(*The Happy Herbivore Cookbook*, p. 162)

Fettuccine Alfredo
  (*The Happy Herbivore Cookbook*, p. 163)
Carrie's Vanilla Chai Cupcakes
  (*The Happy Herbivore Cookbook*, p. 211)

## NEW YEAR'S

Patatas Bravas
  (*Happy Herbivore Abroad*, p. 68)
Cajun Stuffed Mushrooms
  (*Happy Herbivore Abroad*, p. 258)
Pesto-Stuffed Mushrooms
  (*Happy Herbivore Abroad*, p. 99)
Decadent Brownies
  (*Happy Herbivore Abroad*, p. 283)
Taquitos
  (*Happy Herbivore Abroad*, p. 53)
Carolina Casserole
  (*Happy Herbivore Abroad*, p. 265)
Zucchini "Mozzarella" Sticks
  (*Happy Herbivore Light & Lean*, p. 192)

## TAILGATING & APPETIZING PARTIES

Decadent Brownies
  (*Happy Herbivore Abroad*, p. 283)
Blueberry Bundt Cake
  (*Happy Herbivore Abroad*, p. 151)
Cajun Stuffed Mushrooms
  (*Happy Herbivore Abroad*, p. 258)
Nona's Chickpeas
  (*Happy Herbivore Abroad*, p. 51)
Chocolate Glazed Doughnuts
  (*Happy Herbivore Abroad*, p. 155)
"Cheater" Peanut Butter Muffins
  (*Happy Herbivore Light & Lean*, p. 43)
Chocolate Chip Muffins
  (*Happy Herbivore Light & Lean*, p. 44)
Sonoma "Chicken" Salad
  (*Happy Herbivore Light & Lean*, p. 60)

Chili
  (any Happy Herbivore chili recipe will do; see
  all four other cookbooks)
Cornbread
  (in every Happy Herbivore cookbook)
Loaded Mexican Potato
  (*Happy Herbivore Light & Lean*, p. 195)
Tempeh Wings
  (*Happy Herbivore Light & Lean*, p. 204)
Kale Chips
  (*Happy Herbivore Light & Lean*, p. 206)
Baked Potato Samosas
  (*Happy Herbivore Light & Lean*, p. 210)
Spice Cake Surprise
  (*Happy Herbivore Light & Lean*, p. 223)
Granola Bars
  (*Everyday Happy Herbivore*, p. 23)
Masala Burgers
  (*Everyday Happy Herbivore*, p. 83)
Tex-Mex Shepherd's Pie
  (*Everyday Happy Herbivore*, p. 157)
Dijon Rice with Broccoli
  (*Everyday Happy Herbivore*, p. 161)
Creamy Dijon Pasta
  (*Everyday Happy Herbivore*, p. 197)
Tempeh Chili Mac
  (*Everyday Happy Herbivore*, p. 200)
Butter Bean Cookies
  (*Everyday Happy Herbivore*, p. 241)
Apple Fritter Cups
  (*Everyday Happy Herbivore*, p. 248)
Fudge Dip
  (*Everyday Happy Herbivore*, p. 260)
Banana Pudding
  (*Everyday Happy Herbivore*, p. 262)
Apple Crisp Muffins
  (*The Happy Herbivore Cookbook*, p. 40)
Chocolate-Zucchini Muffins
  (*The Happy Herbivore Cookbook*, p. 45)
Southwestern Macaroni Salad
  (*The Happy Herbivore Cookbook*, p. 183)
Low-Country Cucumber Salad
  (*The Happy Herbivore Cookbook*, p. 186)

# ROMANTIC OCCASIONS

Lemony Kale
  (*Happy Herbivore Abroad*, p. 78)
Quick Mole Sauce
  (*Happy Herbivore Abroad*, p. 207)
Decadent Brownies
  (*Happy Herbivore Abroad*, p. 283)
Ruby Chocolate Muffins
  (*Happy Herbivore Light & Lean*, p. 41)
Pesto Burgers
  (*Happy Herbivore Light & Lean*, p. 72)
Chipotle Pasta
  (*Happy Herbivore Light & Lean*, p. 153)
Red Pesto
  (*Happy Herbivore Light & Lean*, p. 156)
Cream Sauce
  (*Happy Herbivore Light & Lean*, p. 157)
Creamy Kale Salad
  (*Happy Herbivore Light & Lean*, p. 180)
Parmesan Greens
  (*Happy Herbivore Light & Lean*, p. 181)
Lemony Asparagus
  (*Happy Herbivore Light & Lean*, p. 183)
Cuban Black Bean Cakes
  (*Everyday Happy Herbivore*, p. 185)
Single-Serving Brownie
  (*The Happy Herbivore Cookbook*, p. 210)

## BRUNCH

## EASTER & PASSOVER

Lemony Kale
(*Happy Herbivore Abroad*, p. 78)
Mama D's Spanakorizo
(*Happy Herbivore Abroad*, p. 120)
Cherry Clafoutis
(*Happy Herbivore Abroad*, p. 152)
Blueberry Bundt Cake
(*Happy Herbivore Abroad*, p. 151)
Crêpes
(*Happy Herbivore Abroad*, p. 158)
Creamy Dijon Gravy
(*Happy Herbivore Abroad*, p. 192)
Tofu Feta
(*Happy Herbivore Abroad*, p. 203)
Blueberry Cornbread Muffins
(*Happy Herbivore Abroad*, p. 249)
Sunshine Muffins
(*Happy Herbivore Abroad*, p. 250)
Lentil Loaf
(*Happy Herbivore Abroad*, p. 257)
Golden Scallion Gravy
(*Happy Herbivore Abroad*, p. 263)
Lemon-Zucchini Muffins
(*Happy Herbivore Light & Lean*, p. 45)
Blueberry Yogurt Muffins
(*Happy Herbivore Light & Lean*, p. 48)
Pineapple-Carrot Muffins
(*Happy Herbivore Light & Lean*, p. 47)
Carrot Soup
(*Happy Herbivore Light & Lean*, p. 105)
Shep's Pie
(*Happy Herbivore Light & Lean*, p. 122)
Waldorf Salad
(*Happy Herbivore Light & Lean*, p. 130)
Creamy Kale Salad
(*Happy Herbivore Light & Lean*, p. 180)
Parmesan Greens
(*Happy Herbivore Light & Lean*, p. 181)
Lemony Asparagus
(*Happy Herbivore Light & Lean*, p. 183)
Lemony Couscous
(*Happy Herbivore Light & Lean*, p. 186)
Cobbler
(*Happy Herbivore Light & Lean*, p. 228)

French Toast Muffins
(*Everyday Happy Herbivore*, p. 53)
Morning Glory Muffins
(*Everyday Happy Herbivore*, p. 54)
Tempeh Meatloaf
(*Everyday Happy Herbivore*, p. 180)
Dijon Asparagus
(*Everyday Happy Herbivore*, p. 226)
Rainbow Greens
(*Everyday Happy Herbivore*, p. 235)
Miso Gravy
(*Everyday Happy Herbivore*, p. 291)
Chickpea Gravy
(*Everyday Happy Herbivore*, p. 287)
Corn Pudding
(*The Happy Herbivore Cookbook*, p. 173)
Carrot Cake Cupcakes
(*The Happy Herbivore Cookbook*, p. 213)

## PICNICS, BARBECUES & OUTDOOR PARTIES

German Sandwich Spread
(*Happy Herbivore Abroad*, p. 52)

German Potato Salad
 (*Happy Herbivore Abroad*, p. 63)
Tabbouleh
 (*Happy Herbivore Abroad*, p. 133)
Orange Teriyaki Rice
 (*Happy Herbivore Abroad*, p. 130)
Pineapple Rice
 (*Happy Herbivore Abroad*, p. 138)
Hummus
 (*Happy Herbivore Abroad*, p. 195)
Pineapple & Black Bean Salsa
 (*Happy Herbivore Abroad*, p. 194)
Chermoula (Moroccan Pesto)
 (*Happy Herbivore Abroad*, p. 197)
AJ's Pico de Gallo
 (*Happy Herbivore Abroad*, p. 202)
Aqua Fresca
 (*Happy Herbivore Abroad*, p. 218)
Gazpacho
 (*Happy Herbivore Abroad*, p. 30)
Lentil Joes
 (*Happy Herbivore Light & Lean*, p. 59)
Meatloaf Bites
 (*Happy Herbivore Light & Lean*, p. 79)
Tempeh Burgers
 (*Happy Herbivore Light & Lean*, p. 77)
"Cheater" Ancient Bowl
 (*Happy Herbivore Light & Lean*, p. 87)
Wraps
 (*Happy Herbivore Light & Lean*, p. 95–100)
Thai Crunch Salad
 (*Happy Herbivore Light & Lean*, p. 139)
BBQ Salad
 (*Happy Herbivore Light & Lean*, p. 133)
Spicy Mango Quinoa Salad
 (*Happy Herbivore Light & Lean*, p. 142)
Smoky Apple Baked Beans
 (*Happy Herbivore Light & Lean*, p. 172)
Chipotle Sweet Potato Salad
 (*Happy Herbivore Light & Lean*, p. 174)
Kale Slaw
 (*Happy Herbivore Light & Lean*, p. 177)
Asian Orange Kale Salad
 (*Happy Herbivore Light & Lean*, p. 179)

Creamy Kale Salad
 (*Happy Herbivore Light & Lean*, p. 180)
Kale Chips
 (*Happy Herbivore Light & Lean*, p. 206)
Cobbler
 (*Happy Herbivore Light & Lean*, p. 228)
Mojito
 (*Happy Herbivore Light & Lean*, p. 253)
Thai Lettuce Wraps
 (*Everyday Happy Herbivore*, p. 130)
Pineapple Sponge Cake
 (*Everyday Happy Herbivore*, p. 256)
Banana Pudding
 (*Everyday Happy Herbivore*, p. 262)
Mushroom Burgers
 (*The Happy Herbivore Cookbook*, p. 89)
Salsa Chickpea Lettuce Wraps
 (*The Happy Herbivore Cookbook*, p. 93)
Smoky Black Bean Wraps
 (*The Happy Herbivore Cookbook*, p. 95)
Steak & Pepper Fajitas
 (*The Happy Herbivore Cookbook*, p. 103)
Southwestern Macaroni Salad
 (*The Happy Herbivore Cookbook*, p. 183)
Tempeh Joes
 (*The Happy Herbivore Cookbook*, p. 111)
Hawaiian Chickpea Teriyaki
 (*The Happy Herbivore Cookbook*, p. 127)

# OTHER HOLIDAYS

## CINCO DE MAYO

Drunken Beans
 (*Happy Herbivore Abroad*, p. 49)
Taquitos
 (*Happy Herbivore Abroad*, p. 53)
Stuffed Poblanos
 (*Happy Herbivore Abroad*, p. 96)
Tostada con Tomate
 (*Happy Herbivore Abroad*, p. 123)

Enchilada Sauce
(*Happy Herbivore Abroad*, p. 201)
AJ's Pico de Gallo
(*Happy Herbivore Abroad*, p. 202)
Quick Mole Sauce
(*Happy Herbivore Abroad*, p. 207)
Tinto de Verano
(*Happy Herbivore Abroad*, p. 215)
Aqua Fresca
(*Happy Herbivore Abroad*, p. 218)
Lentil Taco "Meat"
(*Happy Herbivore Abroad*, p. 43)
Taco Burgers
(*Happy Herbivore Light & Lean*, p. 74)
Chipotle Pasta
(*Happy Herbivore Light & Lean*, p. 153)

## FATHER'S DAY

Bavarian Onion Soup
(*Happy Herbivore Abroad*, p. 33)
"Cheater" Pad Thai
(*Happy Herbivore Abroad*, p. 178–179)
Chili
(in every Happy Herbivore cookbook)
Cornbread
(in every Happy Herbivore cookbook)
Lentil Joes
(*Happy Herbivore Light & Lean*, p. 59)
Thai Tacos
(*Happy Herbivore Light & Lean*, p. 64)
Tempeh Burgers
(*Happy Herbivore Light & Lean*, p. 77)
Cobbler
(*Happy Herbivore Light & Lean*, p. 228)
"Oyster" Po'Boys
(*Everyday Happy Herbivore*, p. 76)

## HALLOWEEN

Pumpkin Pancakes
(*Happy Herbivore Light & Lean*, p. 20)
Pumpkin Muffin
(*Happy Herbivore Light & Lean*, p. 50)
Pumpkin Chili
(*Happy Herbivore Light & Lean*, p. 118)
Pumpkin Spice Latte
(*Happy Herbivore Light & Lean*, p. 256)
Pumpkin Bread
(*The Happy Herbivore Cookbook*, p. 52)

## MARDI GRAS

Cajun Stuffed Mushrooms
(*Happy Herbivore Abroad*, p. 258)
Mardi Gras Red Beans & Rice
(*Everyday Happy Herbivore*, p. 167)
Cajun Chickpea Cakes
(*Everyday Happy Herbivore*, p. 188)
Cajun Potato Salad
(*Everyday Happy Herbivore*, p. 237)
NOLA Gumbo
(*Everyday Happy Herbivore*, p. 108)
Bayou Cornbread
(*Everyday Happy Herbivore*, p. 66)
Cajun Black-Eyed Pea Cakes
(*Everyday Happy Herbivore*, p. 190)
Smoky Cajun Mayo
(*Everyday Happy Herbivore*, p. 267)
Cajun Home Fries
(*The Happy Herbivore Cookbook*, p. 30)
Creole Black-Eyed Peas
(*The Happy Herbivore Cookbook*, p. 121)
Maque Choux
(*The Happy Herbivore Cookbook*, p. 128)
Cajun Meatloaf
(*The Happy Herbivore Cookbook*, p. 141)

Charleston Red Rice
  (*The Happy Herbivore Cookbook*, p. 192)

# MOTHER'S DAY

Crêpes
  (*Happy Herbivore Abroad*, p. 158)
Decadent Brownies
  (*Happy Herbivore Abroad*, p. 283)
Cobbler
  (*Happy Herbivore Light & Lean*, p. 228)
Dark Chocolate Truffles
  (*Happy Herbivore Light & Lean*, p. 230)
Pineapple Sponge Cake
  (*Everyday Happy Herbivore*, p. 256)

# OKTOBERFEST

Bavarian Onion Soup
  (*Happy Herbivore Abroad*, p. 33)
German Potato Salad
  (*Happy Herbivore Abroad*, p. 63)
Radler
  (*Happy Herbivore Abroad*, p. 223)

# ST. PATRICK'S DAY

Colcannon
  (*Happy Herbivore Abroad*, p. 60)
Champ
  (*Happy Herbivore Abroad*, p. 64)
Irish Stew
  (*Happy Herbivore Light & Lean*, p. 113)
Beer Bread
  (*Everyday Happy Herbivore*, p. 69)

# DINNER PARTY MENUS

I love hosting a dinner party! Here are some of my favorite menus for all occasions.

### THE CLASSIC "MEAT AND POTATOES" MENU

Portobello Brisket (p. 86)
Savory Glazed Carrots (p. 123)
roasted mashed potatoes (p. 18)

### A LIGHT SPRING MENU FOR SEAFOOD LOVERS

Crab Cakes with Rémoulade Sauce (p. 53)
corn
asparagus

### A LIGHT SUMMER MENU FOR SEAFOOD LOVERS—PERFECT FOR OUTSIDE!

Crab Cakes with Rémoulade Sauce (p. 53)
Veggie Slaw (p. 132) or Thai Slaw (p. 133)

steamed kale
corn on the cob

### SOUTHERN HOME COOKIN' (COMFORT FOODS) MENU

mac 'n' cheese
green beans
grilled tomatoes, sprinkled with
 AJ's Vegan Parmesan (p. 172)

### CLASSIC ITALIAN MENU

spaghetti with No-Meat Meatballs (p. 91)
salad
crusty bread

### QUICK AND EASY LAST-MINUTE MENU

Mini Soy-Free Quiche (p. 128) or Tofu Quiche
 (see Tofu Scramble, p. 102)
salad or broccoli

## CLASSIC CASUAL SUMMER MENU— EAT OUTSIDE!

Quick Burgers (p. 136)
Oven Fries (p. 77), Baked Onion Rings (p. 77),
  or potato salad
pickle spears

## UPSCALE SUMMER SANDWICH MENU—FOR AL FRESCO DINING!

Portobello Steak (p. 86) sandwiches
  (try adding roasted red bell peppers!)
sweet potato fries
salad

## SUMMER CASUAL BARBECUE MENU

BBQ Sliders (p. 143)
Baked Onion Rings (p. 77)

## SUPER FOODS SANDWICH MENU— EAT OUTSIDE!

Smoky Sweet Potato Burgers (p. 139)
Beet Salad (p. 120) or Thai Slaw (p. 133) or Veggie
  Slaw (p. 132)
kale

## FALL COMFORT MENU

Portobello Pot Roast (p. 30)
cauliflower mashed potatoes (p. 18)
Brussels sprouts

## FALL SOUTHERN "COMFORT FOODS" MENU

Portobello Pot Roast (p. 30)
Dijon mashed potatoes (p. 18)
Creamed Spinach (see Creamed Kale, p. 65)

## OKTOBERFEST MENU

Soft Pretzels (p. 159)
Carrot Hot Dogs (p. 148), topped with German
  mustard, sauerkraut, onions
Potato Salad (p. 123) or Cajun Potato Salad (p. 62)

## CLASSIC DINNER PARTY MENU

vegan meatloaf (such as Cajun Tempeh Meatloaf, p. 62
  or Meatloaf Bites, p. 51)
mashed potatoes (p. 18)
gravy
green beans

## LIGHT ASIAN-INSPIRED MENU

Spring Rolls (p. 52)
"Cheater" Spicy Peanut Noodles (p. 136)
edamame

## CLASSIC COLD-WEATHER COMFORT MENU

chili (such as Chili Sans Carne, p. 72 or Rustic Chili, p. 70)
Cornbread (p. 19)

## LIGHT SOUP & SALAD MENU

Cream of Broccoli Soup (p. 124)
crusty bread
Beet Salad (p. 120) over spinach

## A TASTE OF AFRICA MENU

West African Peanut Stew (p. 33)
couscous
roasted carrots

# GLOSSARY OF INGREDIENTS

## agave nectar

Pronounced ah-*gah*-vay, agave nectar is a natural, unrefined sweetener with a consistency similar to honey.

## black salt

Black salt is also called *kala namak*. Not to be confused with Hawaiian black lava salt.

## coconut aminos

A soy-free substitute for soy sauce.

## liquid smoke

Found in most supermarkets, liquid smoke is smoke condensation captured in water. It looks like low-sodium soy sauce but smells like barbecue.

## miso

Found in the refrigerated food section of health food stores and Asian supermarkets, miso is usually made from soybeans, although it can also be made from rice, barley, wheat, or chickpeas.

## nondairy milk

Soy milk, rice milk, hemp milk, oat milk, and almond milk are just some of the many kinds of nondairy milk on the market.

## nutritional yeast

Nutritional yeast is a deactivated yeast, meaning it doesn't make breads rise the way active yeast does. It also gives food a cheesy flavor. You can find nutritional yeast in health food stores and some Krogers. I recommend Red Star or Bragg's brands.

## poultry seasoning

Poultry seasoning is a blend of basil, rosemary, thyme, sage, marjoram, and oregano, but other herbs may be included. Avoid buying powdered poultry spice or chicken spice rubs, which can be salty. In a pinch, substitute Italian seasoning.

## powdered sugar

Also called confectioners' sugar, powdered sugar is fine and powder-like. You can make

your own by combining 1 cup of raw sugar with two tbsp of cornstarch in your food processor and letting the motor run until a fine powder is formed.

## pumpkin pie spice

A blend of cinnamon, ginger, cloves, and nutmeg.

## pure maple syrup

Pure maple syrup is a delicious natural, unrefined sweetener. Imitation maple syrups and pancake syrups cannot be substituted without sacrificing taste and quality.

## pure pumpkin

Pure pumpkin is different from pumpkin pie mix. (Don't use that.) You want canned pure pumpkin or the insides of an actual pumpkin. In a pinch, you can substitute canned sweet potato or butternut squash.

## tamari

Interchangeable with low-sodium soy sauce in recipes, tamari is similar to low-sodium soy sauce, but thicker and usually gluten-free.

## vegan chocolate chips

Many semisweet chocolate chips are unintentionally vegan. Ghirardelli is my favorite brand.

## vegan yogurt

Yogurt made from soy, rice, almond, or coconut milk instead of dairy. If you have a dairy allergy or are vegan, make sure the cultures are not from dairy, either.

## vital wheat gluten

You can find vital wheat gluten in the baking section of health food stores or online. For a gluten-free substitute, use Orgran's Gluten Free Gluten Substitute.

# KITCHEN PREP LINGO

## almost combined/just combined

Do not completely combine ingredients. With batter, some flour should still be visible for it to be almost combined. To be just combined, stir it just a little bit more—ingredients should be mixed together and incorporated, but barely. Use as few strokes as possible. (Compare with *blend*.)

## blend

Stir to incorporate all ingredients until they are well combined and the mix is homogenous.

## chop

Cut ingredient into bite-size pieces; uniform cuts are not necessary, and size is relatively unimportant (it's more of a personal preference).

## cream

Beat the ingredients with an electric mixer until they are well combined and have a creamy consistency. This also can be done by hand with a spatula.

## crumble

Break the ingredient apart into smaller pieces. With tofu, break the tofu apart until it resembles ricotta or feta cheese.

## fold

Gently stir a single ingredient into a mixture, such as muffin batter, with a spatula or large spoon until just combined.

## mince

Chop ingredients into very small pieces, ⅛ inch or smaller.

## salt and pepper to taste

½ tsp of salt and ¼ tsp of pepper is usually a good starting point for recipes that serve at least two. Reduce salt if you're using ingredients with sodium, such as canned goods or low-sodium soy sauce. Double as necessary to achieve your preferred taste.

## stir

Use a circular motion, clockwise or counterclockwise, to move or incorporate ingredients.

# METRIC CONVERSIONS

### Abbreviation Key
tsp = teaspoon
tbsp = tablespoon
dsp = dessert spoon

| U.S. STANDARD | U.K. |
|---|---|
| ¼ tsp | ¼ tsp (scant) |
| ½ tsp | ½ tsp (scant) |
| ¾ tsp | ½ tsp (rounded) |
| 1 tsp | ¾ tsp (slightly rounded) |
| 1 tbsp | 2½ tsp |
| ¼ cup | ¼ cup minus 1 dsp |
| ⅓ cup | ¼ cup plus 1 tsp |
| ½ cup | ⅓ cup plus 2 dsp |
| ⅔ cup | ½ cup plus 1 tbsp |
| ¾ cup | ½ cup plus 2 tbsp |
| 1 cup | ¾ cup plus 2 dsp |

# ACKNOWLEDGMENTS

Life is a celebration and I feel very fortunate to share mine with my family, friends, and fans (called "Herbies"), who continually support me and make my life sweet.

I would also like to acknowledge my publisher and the entire BenBella Books team. It takes many hands to make these books happen and I couldn't do it without them!

A special thank you to my husband, Scott Nixon, my partner in life, business, and love. Each day with you is a gift. I could not do what I do without you.

Jackie Sobon, Natala Constantine, Neely Roberts, and Ira Mintz, thank you for your beautiful pictures that bring this book to life.

I would also like to stand up and applaud my past and present team at Happy Herbivore during the creation of this book: Carly Verble, Lindsey Pechal, Alison Rood, and Jamee Dyches. Behind every successful person is a supportive team. You make it all possible!

To my parents, Richard and Lenore Shay, I continue to be the proudest daughter in the world. Thank you for the support, the work you do for Happy Herbivore, and having what is often a thankless job—being a parent to me. Thank you. Thank you. Thank you. I love you (and so do the Herbies!).

To my entire family, especially my late grandmother, Ann Pentasuglio, and my aunts, Carol Stalica and Joan Miro, thank you for giving me the moments, memories, and experiences that I drew upon and used to shape my recipes in this book. Because of you, cooking has become how I express love. With gratitude.

Lastly, I could never thank my amazing testers (who took on the collective name of "Mad Hat Mangoes") enough:

- Dana Strickland
- Gin Stafford
- Pragati Sawhney Coder
- Pam Wertz
- Katharina Ikels
- Ashley and Michael Nebel
- Courtney Hardy
- Kim Michael
- Sue Bair
- Kimberly Roy
- Jenny Calderon
- Dirk Wethington
- The Treanor Family
- Becky Soubeyrand
- Kait Scalisi
- Amanda Thompson
- Lisa Canada and Family
- Gayle Pollick
- MarieRoxanne Veinotte
- Jennifer Kent

My cookbooks could not exist without your hard work and dedication.

# ABOUT THE AUTHOR

**Lindsay S. Nixon** is the best-selling author of the Happy Herbivore cookbook series: *The Happy Herbivore Cookbook* (2011), *Everyday Happy Herbivore* (2011), *Happy Herbivore Abroad* (2012), *Happy Herbivore Light & Lean* (2013), *The Happy Herbivore Guide to Plant-Based Living* (2014, e-book only), and now *Happy Herbivore Holidays & Gatherings*. Nixon has sold over 200,000 copies of her cookbooks.

Nixon has been featured on the Food Network and *The Dr. Oz Show*, and she has spoken at Google's Pittsburgh office about health, plant-based food, and her success. She is also a teaching professor at the Center for Nutrition Studies at eCornell and her recipes have been featured in the *New York Times*, *Vegetarian Times* magazine, *Shape* magazine, *Bust*, *Women's Health*, WebMD, and numerous other publications. Nixon's work has also been praised and endorsed by notable leaders in the field of nutrition, including Dr. T. Colin Campbell, Dr. Caldwell B. Esselstyn Jr., Dr. Neal Barnard, Dr. John McDougall, and Dr. Pam Popper.

A rising star in the culinary world, Nixon is recognized for her ability to use everyday ingredients to create healthy, low-fat recipes that taste just as delicious as they are nutritious. Learn more about Nixon and try some of her recipes on her award-winning blog happyherbivore.com. You can also try her 7-Day Meal Plans at getmealplans.com.

Other cookbooks
by Lindsay S. Nixon,
brought to you by BenBella Books

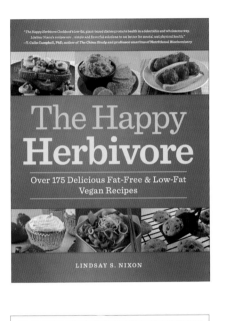

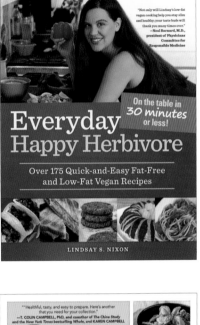

And coming soon: *The Happy Herbivore
Guide to Plant-Based Living* (available May 2015)

# Recipe Index

AJ's Vegan Parmesan

# RECIPE INDEX

Hot Chocolate Muffins

Cowboy Beans

White Bean Gravy

West African Peanut Stew

# RECIPE INDEX

# Full Index

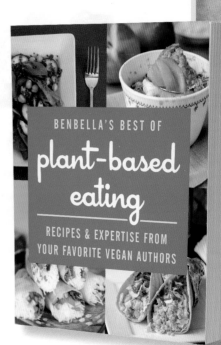

CHERRY QUINOA SALAD

TRICOLORED VEGETABLE
PASTA WITH SUN-DRIED
MARINARA AND
CASHEW CHEESE

CAULIFLOWER HOT WINGS

BUDDHA LENTIL BURGER

MEDITERRANEAN CHARD

BLUEBERRY BUNDT CAKE

# WITH NEARLY 50 RECIPES FROM

*The China Study Cookbook* | *The Happy Herbivore series*
*Better Than Vegan* | *Blissful Bites*
*The Best Green Smoothies on the Planet*
*The HappyCow Cookbook* | *Jazzy Vegetarian Classics*
*The PlantPure Nation Cookbook* | *YumUniverse*

## AND SELECTIONS FROM

*Whole* | *The Low-Carb Fraud*
*Food Over Medicine* | *Healthy Eating, Healthy World*

11/14-H